BEYOND BOUNDARIES

A Guide to Personal, Professional, Social and Spiritual Growth

Dr. Mukesh Aggarwal

PREFACE

In an ever-evolving world, boundaries are often perceived as limitations—barriers that confine us within a defined space. However, my journey has revealed that boundaries are not merely obstacles but opportunities for growth and transformation. The essence of this book, Beyond Boundaries: A Guide to Personal, Professional, Social, and Spiritual Growth, is to challenge conventional perceptions and explore how breaking through these boundaries can lead to profound personal and collective advancement.

As a lifelong advocate for holistic development, I have witnessed firsthand the remarkable transformations that occur when individuals dare to step beyond their comfort zones. This book is a culmination of insights garnered from years of professional practice, personal experiences, and countless interactions with individuals from diverse walks of life. It is designed to serve as a compass for those seeking to navigate their journey of self-discovery, professional excellence, social impact, and spiritual enlightenment.

The journey of transcending boundaries is not one of simple change but of deep, often challenging, exploration. It involves embracing change, confronting fears, nurturing creativity, fostering resilience, and finding purpose. Through the chapters, you will encounter practical tools, inspiring stories, and transformative case studies that illuminate the path to breaking free from limitations and achieving a richer, more fulfilled existence.

Each section of this book—Personal Growth Beyond Boundaries, Professional Excellence Beyond Boundaries, Social Impact Beyond Boundaries, and Spiritual Enlightenment Beyond Boundaries—offers a unique perspective on overcoming barriers and unlocking potential. My goal is to inspire you to challenge your own boundaries and to equip you with the knowledge and tools to forge a path of growth that is uniquely yours.

This book is more than just a guide; it is an invitation to embark on a journey of discovery and empowerment. I encourage you to approach each chapter with an open mind and a willingness to explore new horizons. As you read and reflect, may you find the courage to break through your own boundaries and embrace the limitless possibilities that await you.

Thank you for joining me on this journey. I hope that Beyond Boundaries inspires you to live a life of purpose, creativity, and fulfillment, reaching beyond what you once thought possible.

Warm regards,

Dr. Mukesh Aggarwal

ACKNOWLEDGEMENTS

Writing Beyond Boundaries: A Guide to Personal, Professional, Social, and Spiritual Growth has been a deeply rewarding endeavor, and I am profoundly grateful to those who have supported and inspired me throughout this journey.

Firstly, I extend my heartfelt thanks to my family, whose unwavering support and encouragement have been my bedrock. Your belief in me and in this project has provided the strength and motivation needed to see it through.

To my colleagues and mentors, your invaluable insights and guidance have shaped the content of this book. Your wisdom and experience have been instrumental in crafting a narrative that is both practical and inspiring.

A special thank you to the countless individuals whose personal stories and transformative journeys have enriched this book. Your willingness to share your experiences has made this work a testament to the power of overcoming boundaries and achieving growth.

To the research and academic communities, I appreciate your contributions to the knowledge base that underpins this book. Your dedication to advancing understanding has been a source of inspiration.

My deepest gratitude goes to my editorial team and the publishing staff who have worked diligently to bring this book to life. Your expertise and attention to detail have been crucial in translating my vision into reality.

Lastly, to the readers, thank you for your curiosity and commitment to personal and collective growth. It is my hope that this book serves as a valuable resource on your own journey of breaking through boundaries and discovering new possibilities.

With sincere appreciation,

Dr. Mukesh Aggarwal

INTRODUCTION
Defining Boundaries

Chapter 1

THE CONCEPT OF BOUNDARIES

Boundaries are fundamental to personal, professional, social, and spiritual growth. They act as invisible lines that delineate our physical, emotional, and psychological spaces, ensuring that we maintain healthy and respectful relationships with ourselves and others. Understanding and establishing boundaries is essential for achieving balance, fostering self-respect, and nurturing meaningful connections.

Personal Boundaries

Personal boundaries are about self-care and self-respect. They involve recognizing your limits and ensuring that others respect them. Personal boundaries protect your mental health, allowing you to say no without feeling guilty and to take time for yourself without feeling selfish.

Physical Boundaries: These pertain to your personal space and physical touch. They define how close others can get to you and what kind of physical interactions are acceptable. Respecting physical boundaries is crucial for feeling safe and comfortable.

Emotional Boundaries: These involve separating your emotions and responsibilities from those of others. Emotional boundaries help you manage your feelings, avoid overextending yourself emotionally, and prevent taking on others' emotional burdens.

Time Boundaries: These concern how you allocate your time. Time boundaries are vital for ensuring that you can balance work, personal life, and leisure. They involve setting limits on work hours, social engagements, and personal time to avoid burnout.

Professional Boundaries

Professional boundaries are essential for maintaining a healthy and productive work environment. They help define appropriate interactions, responsibilities, and expectations within the workplace.

Role Boundaries: These clarify your responsibilities and the extent of your duties. They help prevent role confusion and ensure that you and your colleagues understand each other's tasks and limits.

Work-Life Balance: Establishing boundaries between work and personal life is crucial. This includes setting specific work hours, taking breaks, and not allowing work to intrude on personal time. A healthy work-life balance is key to long-term productivity and well-being.

Interpersonal Boundaries: These involve maintaining professional relationships with colleagues and clients. They include appropriate communication, respecting personal space, and avoiding conflicts of interest. Professional boundaries ensure a respectful and efficient work environment.

Social Boundaries

Social boundaries are about managing relationships with friends, family, and acquaintances. They help you navigate social interactions and maintain healthy, respectful connections.

Communication Boundaries: These define how you communicate with others and what topics are acceptable. They help prevent misunderstandings, gossip, and inappropriate conversations. Clear communication boundaries foster mutual respect and understanding.

Relationship Boundaries: These involve setting limits on the nature and extent of your relationships. They help you manage expectations and avoid over-committing to social obligations. Healthy relationship boundaries ensure that your social interactions are supportive and enriching.

Privacy Boundaries: These pertain to your personal information and space. They involve deciding what you share with others and what you keep private. Respecting privacy boundaries is essential for building trust and maintaining personal integrity.

Spiritual Boundaries

Spiritual boundaries are about defining your beliefs, values, and practices. They help you stay true to your spiritual path and respect others' beliefs.

Faith Boundaries: These involve respecting your own and others' religious or spiritual beliefs. They include the right to practice your faith freely and to engage in spiritual activities without interference.

Ethical Boundaries: These define your moral and ethical principles. They help you make decisions aligned with your values and maintain integrity in your actions. Ethical boundaries are crucial for personal and spiritual growth.

Practice Boundaries: These involve setting limits on your spiritual practices and rituals. They ensure that you have time and space for spiritual activities, such as meditation, prayer, or reflection. Practice boundaries help you stay connected to your spiritual self.

Conclusion

Understanding and establishing boundaries is a lifelong process that requires self-awareness, communication, and respect. Boundaries are not barriers but essential tools for fostering healthy relationships, achieving personal and professional growth, and nurturing spiritual well-being. By recognizing and honoring our boundaries and those of others, we create a harmonious and balanced life, paving the way for continuous growth and fulfillment.

Chapter 2

THE IMPORTANCE OF BOUNDARIES IN HUMAN LIFE

Introduction

Boundaries are often perceived as limitations, yet they play a crucial role in fostering personal, professional, social, and spiritual growth. This chapter delves into the significance of boundaries, exploring how they shape our lives, enhance our relationships, and contribute to overall well-being.

Personal Boundaries

1. Self-Respect and Self-Care

Personal boundaries are fundamental to self-respect and self-care. They define what is acceptable behavior from others and what is not. Setting clear boundaries helps in maintaining a healthy relationship with oneself, ensuring that one's needs and values are honored.

Example: Consider the practice of saying no to additional work when your plate is already full. This not only prevents burnout but also signals to others that you value your time and energy.

2. Emotional Well-Being

Boundaries protect our emotional well-being. They help us manage our emotions by preventing others from imposing their feelings or expectations onto us. This autonomy is vital for maintaining mental health and fostering resilience.

Anita a dedicated professional realized that constant availability to her colleagues was draining her. By setting specific hours for work-related communications, she reclaimed her evenings for relaxation and family time, significantly improving her emotional health.

Professional Boundaries

1. Enhancing Productivity

In the workplace, boundaries are essential for productivity. They help in managing time effectively, ensuring that tasks are completed efficiently without unnecessary interruptions. Clear professional boundaries also prevent work from encroaching on personal life, fostering a better work-life balance.

Story: Raj, a project manager, instituted a policy of no meetings after 4 PM. This boundary allowed his team to have uninterrupted time for focused work, leading to a noticeable increase in productivity.

2. Professional Relationships

Boundaries in professional relationships maintain respect and prevent conflicts. They ensure that interactions remain professional and that personal issues do not interfere with work dynamics.

Naveen a team leader, faced challenges with a colleague who often brought personal problems into the workplace. By gently reinforcing the need to separate personal issues from professional responsibilities, Naveen maintained a positive and productive work environment.

Social Boundaries

1. Healthy Relationships

Social boundaries are key to healthy relationships. They define the limits within which interactions occur, preventing overstepping and ensuring mutual respect. Clear boundaries help in avoiding misunderstandings and conflicts, fostering trust and respect among friends and family.

Analogy: Think of social boundaries as the rules of a game. Just as rules ensure fair play and enjoyment, boundaries ensure that relationships are nurturing and respectful.

2. Personal Space

Respecting personal space is a fundamental social boundary. It involves recognizing and honoring others' need for privacy and autonomy, which is essential for harmonious coexistence.

Statistical Insight: Studies have shown that individuals with clearly defined social boundaries report higher levels of satisfaction in their relationships and overall life.

Spiritual Boundaries

1. Spiritual Growth

Spiritual boundaries help in nurturing one's spiritual journey. They involve setting limits on external influences that might hinder spiritual practices or beliefs. By protecting one's spiritual space, individuals can pursue their path with clarity and focus.

Metaphor: Consider spiritual boundaries as a garden fence. It keeps out weeds and pests, allowing the plants inside to flourish and grow.

2. Respect for Diverse Beliefs

Respecting others' spiritual boundaries fosters a culture of tolerance and understanding. It acknowledges the diversity of beliefs and practices, promoting peaceful coexistence and mutual respect.

Case Study: In a multicultural workplace, Ramesh, an HR manager, created a policy allowing flexible break times for employees to observe their religious practices. This boundary respected individual beliefs while maintaining workplace harmony.

Conclusion

Boundaries are not barriers; they are essential frameworks that support personal integrity, professional efficiency, social harmony, and spiritual growth. By understanding and respecting boundaries, we can lead more balanced, fulfilling, and harmonious lives. In the journey of growth and self-discovery, boundaries are the markers that guide us, ensuring we navigate our paths with respect, clarity, and purpose.

Chapter 3

THE VISION BEHIND BEYOND BOUNDARIES

The journey of growth, both personal and professional, often requires us to break through the invisible barriers that confine us. These barriers can be self-imposed limitations, societal norms, or even fears and uncertainties about the future. The concept of 'Beyond Boundaries' emerged as a beacon for those seeking to transcend these constraints and achieve a holistic form of development.

The Genesis of the Vision

The idea for 'Beyond Boundaries' was born out of a realization that true growth encompasses more than just professional success or personal well-being. It is about integrating these aspects with social and spiritual dimensions to create a balanced and fulfilling life. This comprehensive approach ensures that individuals do not excel in one area at the expense of another but rather achieve a harmonious growth that is sustainable and enriching.

Dr. Mukesh Aggarwal, a renowned expert in holistic health and personal development, conceptualized 'Beyond Boundaries' as a platform to share knowledge, inspire change, and foster a community of growth-oriented individuals. His extensive experience in Ayurveda and social work provided a unique perspective that blends ancient wisdom with contemporary insights.

Personal Growth: The Foundation

At the heart of 'Beyond Boundaries' lies the belief that personal growth is the cornerstone of all other forms of development. Personal growth involves self-awareness, emotional intelligence, and the continuous pursuit of knowledge and skills. It is about understanding one's strengths and weaknesses, setting meaningful goals, and cultivating habits that lead to a more fulfilling life.

Dr. Aggarwal emphasizes the importance of mindfulness, self-reflection, and resilience in the personal growth journey. These elements help individuals navigate life's challenges, maintain a positive outlook, and build a strong foundation for further growth.

Professional Growth: Beyond Career Success

Professional growth is often associated with climbing the corporate ladder or achieving financial success. However, 'Beyond Boundaries' advocates for a broader perspective that includes job satisfaction, work-life balance, and alignment with one's values and passions.

In today's fast-paced world, it is easy to lose sight of what truly matters in the pursuit of professional success. Dr. Aggarwal's approach encourages individuals to seek meaningful work that not only provides financial stability but also fulfills their passions and contributes to their overall well-being.

Social Growth: Building Meaningful Connections

Humans are inherently social beings, and our interactions with others significantly impact our growth. Social growth involves building and maintaining healthy relationships, contributing to the community, and developing a sense of empathy and compassion.

'Beyond Boundaries' emphasizes the importance of effective communication, active listening, and the ability to understand and respect diverse perspectives. By fostering a sense of community and belonging, individuals can create supportive networks that enhance their personal and professional lives.

Spiritual Growth: The Inner Journey

Spiritual growth is often misunderstood as being solely related to religious practices. However, in the context of 'Beyond Boundaries,' it is about finding a deeper sense of purpose, meaning, and connection to something greater than oneself.

Dr. Aggarwal encourages individuals to explore their spirituality through various means, such as meditation, nature, art, and introspection. This inner journey helps individuals align their actions with their core values, leading to a more purposeful and content life.

Integration: The Holistic Approach

The true essence of 'Beyond Boundaries' lies in the integration of personal, professional, social, and spiritual growth. This holistic approach ensures that individuals are not compartmentalizing their lives but are instead creating a balanced and harmonious existence.

By breaking down the boundaries that separate these aspects, individuals can achieve a state of flow where each area of their life supports and enhances the others. This integrated growth leads to a more resilient, adaptable, and fulfilled individual.

The Future of Beyond Boundaries

The vision for 'Beyond Boundaries' is not just limited to individual growth. It aims to create a ripple effect that extends to communities, organizations, and society at large. By empowering individuals to break through their boundaries, Dr. Aggarwal hopes to foster a culture of continuous improvement, empathy, and holistic well-being.

As the 'Beyond Boundaries' movement grows, it will continue to evolve, incorporating new insights, technologies, and methodologies to support the ever-changing needs of individuals and society. The ultimate goal is to create a world where growth is not just about reaching new heights but also about deepening our roots and expanding our horizons in all dimensions of life.

Conclusion

The vision behind **'Beyond Boundaries'** is a call to action for anyone seeking a more fulfilling and balanced life. It is an invitation to explore the uncharted territories of personal, professional, social, and spiritual growth. By embracing this holistic approach, individuals can break free from their limitations and embark on a transformative journey towards a brighter, more enriched future.

PART I
Personal Growth beyond Boundaries

Chapter 4

EMBRACE CHANGE

Introduction

Change is the only constant in life, yet it is often met with resistance and fear. Embracing change is a crucial aspect of personal growth, allowing us to expand our horizons, adapt to new situations, and ultimately become more resilient individuals. In this chapter, we will explore the nature of change, the reasons behind our resistance to it, and strategies to embrace change effectively.

Understanding Change

Change comes in many forms, from the small, everyday alterations in our routines to significant life events such as career transitions, relationships, or health challenges. These changes can be voluntary, like deciding to pursue a new hobby, or involuntary, such as losing a job or facing a health crisis. Understanding that change is an inevitable part of life helps we prepare mentally and emotionally for its arrival.

The Nature of Resistance

Our resistance to change is rooted in our desire for stability and predictability. The human brain is wired to seek comfort in familiarity, as it conserves energy and reduces uncertainty. Change often triggers a fear response, as it challenges our sense of control and can evoke anxiety about the unknown. Acknowledging these natural tendencies is the first step towards overcoming resistance.

The Benefits of Embracing Change

1. **Personal Growth:** Embracing change pushes us out of our comfort zones, encouraging us to develop new skills and perspectives. It fosters creativity and innovation, as we are forced to find new solutions to emerging challenges.

2. **Resilience:** Adapting to change strengthens our resilience, enabling us to bounce back from setbacks more effectively. This resilience builds confidence and prepares us for future changes.

3. **Opportunities:** Change often brings new opportunities that we might not have considered before. By being open to change, we can seize these opportunities and enhance our personal and professional lives.

4. **Flexibility:** Embracing change cultivates flexibility, making it easier to adapt to various situations. This flexibility is essential in a rapidly evolving world, where the ability to pivot and adjust is crucial for success.

Strategies to Embrace Change

1. **Mindset Shift:** Adopting a growth mindset, where challenges are seen as opportunities for learning and development, is key to embracing change. This mindset helps us view change as a positive force rather than a threat.

2. **Self-Awareness:** Reflecting on past experiences with change can provide valuable insights into how we react and adapt. Understanding our triggers and responses helps us prepare for future changes.

3. **Acceptance:** Accepting that change is a natural part of life reduces resistance. This acceptance involves letting go of the need to control every aspect of our lives and trusting in our ability to navigate change successfully.

4. **Support Systems:** Building a strong support network of friends, family, and mentors can provide emotional and practical assistance during times of change. Sharing experiences and seeking advice can alleviate feelings of isolation and fear.

5. **Continuous Learning:** Embracing a lifelong learning attitude equips us with the skills and knowledge needed to adapt to new situations. This proactive approach ensures we remain relevant and capable in an ever-changing world.

Case Study: Sarah's Career Transition

Sarah had worked in the same industry for over a decade. When her company underwent restructuring, she found herself facing an unexpected job loss. Initially, Sarah felt overwhelmed and fearful of the unknown. However, she decided to view this change as an opportunity to explore new career paths. She enrolled in online courses, networked with professionals in different fields, and eventually transitioned into a role that aligned with her passions. By embracing change, Sarah discovered a more fulfilling career and developed a stronger sense of resilience.

Personal Reflections

Think about a time when you faced a significant change. How did you react initially, and how did you eventually adapt? What lessons did you learn from this experience? Reflecting on these questions can provide valuable insights into your relationship with change and how you can better embrace it in the future.

Conclusion

Embracing change is a vital component of personal growth beyond boundaries. By understanding the nature of change, recognizing our resistance, and adopting strategies to navigate it, we can transform challenges into opportunities for growth and development. Embracing change not only enhances our resilience and flexibility but also opens doors to new and exciting possibilities. As we continue on our journey of personal growth, let us welcome change as a trusted companion, guiding us towards a more enriched and fulfilling life.

Chapter 5

THE NATURE OF CHANGE

Introduction

Change is an integral part of the human experience, influencing every aspect of our lives. Understanding the nature of change is essential for personal growth, as it helps us navigate life's transitions with grace and resilience. This chapter delves into the fundamental aspects of change, exploring its types, underlying causes, and the psychological impact it has on individuals.

Types of Change

Change manifests in various forms, each with its own implications and challenges. Recognizing these different types can help us better prepare for and respond to change.

1. **Personal Change:** This involves shifts in our thoughts, behaviors, and emotions. Personal change can be voluntary, such as adopting a new habit, or involuntary, like experiencing a significant life event. It is often driven by a desire for self-improvement or as a response to external circumstances.

2. **Professional Change:** Changes in the workplace, including career transitions, promotions, or organizational restructuring, fall under this category. Professional change can be exciting yet challenging, requiring adaptability and continuous learning.

3. **Social Change:** This encompasses changes in our relationships and social dynamics. Moving to a new city, forming new friendships, or adjusting to changes in family structure are examples. Social change can significantly impact our support systems and sense of belonging.

4. **Environmental Change:** This refers to changes in our physical surroundings, such as moving to a new home or adapting to new cultural environments. Environmental change often requires us to adjust our routines and perspectives.

5. **Global Change:** On a larger scale, global changes like technological advancements, economic shifts, and societal transformations influence our lives in profound ways. Staying informed and adaptable is crucial to thriving in a rapidly changing world.

Causes of Change

Understanding the causes of change helps us anticipate and manage its effects more effectively. Some common drivers of change include:

1. **Technological Advancements:** Innovations in technology continually reshape how we live and work. From the advent of the internet to the rise of artificial intelligence, technological change demands adaptability and lifelong learning.

2. **Economic Factors:** Economic shifts, such as recessions, booms, and globalization, can lead to significant changes in our professional and personal lives. Economic change often necessitates financial planning and career flexibility.

3. **Social Movements:** Changes in societal values and norms, driven by social movements and cultural shifts, influence our behavior and interactions. Being aware of these changes helps us navigate evolving social landscapes.

4. **Life Events:** Personal milestones like marriage, parenthood, and retirement bring about significant changes. These events often require emotional adjustment and planning.

5. **Health:** Changes in our physical and mental health can dramatically alter our lives. Adapting to health-related changes involves resilience and proactive self-care.

Psychological Impact of Change

Change can evoke a range of emotions, from excitement and anticipation to fear and anxiety. Understanding the psychological impact of change can help us manage our responses more effectively.

1. **Fear of the Unknown:** One of the most common reactions to change is fear of the unknown. Uncertainty about the future can

lead to anxiety and stress. Acknowledging this fear is the first step towards overcoming it.

2. **Loss of Control:** Change often involves a perceived loss of control over our circumstances. This can lead to feelings of helplessness and frustration. Regaining a sense of control through proactive planning and decision-making is essential.

3. **Resistance:** Our natural inclination to resist change stems from a desire for stability and familiarity. Resistance can manifest as procrastination, denial, or avoidance. Recognizing and addressing resistance helps us move forward.

4. **Adaptation:** Over time, humans are remarkably adaptable. Even significant changes become more manageable as we adjust our expectations and routines. Embracing a mindset of adaptability enhances our resilience.

5. **Growth and Transformation:** Despite its challenges, change often leads to personal growth and transformation. Navigating change successfully can boost our confidence, expand our perspectives, and enhance our capabilities.

Case Study: Arun Midlife Career Change

Arun had spent two decades in the corporate world when he felt a growing dissatisfaction with his career. The idea of switching to a completely different field in his mid-40s seemed daunting. However, after much contemplation, he decided to pursue his passion for teaching. The transition was challenging, requiring additional education and a significant lifestyle adjustment. Despite the initial hurdles, Arun found immense satisfaction and fulfillment in his new role. His experience highlights how embracing change can lead to profound personal growth and happiness.

Personal Reflections

Consider a significant change you have experienced in your life. How did you react initially, and what strategies helped you adapt? Reflecting on these experiences can provide valuable insights into your relationship with change and your capacity for resilience.

Conclusion

Understanding the nature of change is a foundational aspect of personal growth beyond boundaries. By recognizing the different types and causes of change, and acknowledging its psychological impact, we can better navigate life's transitions. Embracing change, despite its challenges, opens the door to personal transformation, resilience, and a deeper understanding of ourselves and the world around us. As we continue on our journey of personal growth, let us welcome change as a catalyst for progress and self-discovery.

Chapter 6

OVERCOMING FEAR OF THE UNKNOWN

In the grand tapestry of life, one thread that often hinders our growth and potential is the fear of the unknown. This fear can manifest in various aspects of our lives, paralyzing us with indecision and preventing us from seizing new opportunities. To achieve personal growth beyond boundaries, it is essential to confront and overcome this fear.

Understanding the Fear of the Unknown

The fear of the unknown, or xenophobia, is a deeply ingrained human emotion. It stems from our evolutionary past, where the unknown could pose potential threats to our survival. This primal instinct, while protective, often limits our ability to explore new horizons in the modern world. Understanding this fear is the first step towards conquering it.

Recognizing the Impact

Fear of the unknown can impact various facets of our lives. It can prevent us from changing careers, moving to new places, or even forming new relationships. This fear often manifests as anxiety, stress, and procrastination, creating a cycle of stagnation and missed opportunities.

Consider the story of Madhurima, a talented graphic designer who spent years in a job she found unfulfilling. Her fear of leaving the familiar confines of her current job for the uncertainty of freelancing kept her from pursuing her passion. It wasn't until she confronted this fear that she discovered a thriving career that aligned with her true calling.

Strategies for Overcoming Fear

Embrace a Growth Mindset

A growth mindset, as coined by psychologist Carol Dweck, is the belief that abilities and intelligence can be developed through dedication and hard work. Embracing this mindset shifts our perspective from fearing the unknown to viewing it as an opportunity for growth and learning.

Take Small Steps

Overcoming fear doesn't require drastic changes overnight. Start with small, manageable steps. If public speaking terrifies you, begin by speaking in front of a mirror, then to a small group of friends, gradually increasing your audience. Each step builds confidence and reduces fear.

Visualize Success

Visualization is a powerful tool used by athletes and successful individuals. Picture yourself successfully navigating the unknown. Visualize the positive outcomes and the emotions associated with your success. This mental rehearsal can reduce anxiety and build confidence.

Seek Support

Surround yourself with supportive individuals who encourage and believe in your potential. A mentor or a supportive friend can provide guidance, offer perspective, and hold you accountable as you navigate uncharted territories.

Reframe Failure

Fear of the unknown is often intertwined with the fear of failure. Reframe failure as a learning experience rather than a setback. Thomas Edison famously said, "I have not failed. I've just found 10,000 ways that won't work." Each failure brings you closer to success.

Educate Yourself

Knowledge is a powerful antidote to fear. Research and gather information about the unknown. The more informed you are, the less intimidating it becomes. If you're considering a career change, for instance, talk to people in the field, attend workshops, and read extensively.

The Power of Letting Go

One of the most profound steps in overcoming fear of the unknown is learning to let go of the need for control. Life is inherently uncertain, and attempting to control every aspect can lead to frustration and anxiety. Embrace the uncertainty and view it as a natural part of life's journey.

Consider the analogy of a river. The water flows naturally, encountering obstacles along the way but finding its path regardless. When we let go and allow ourselves to flow with lives currents, we often find ourselves in places we never imagined, enriched by experiences we never anticipated.

Personal Anecdote: Embracing the Unknown

In my own journey, I faced a pivotal moment where the fear of the unknown loomed large. Transitioning from a stable corporate job to pursue my passion for writing was a daunting decision. The uncertainty of success, financial instability, and the fear of judgment weighed heavily on me.

However, by applying the strategies outlined above, I took the leap. The journey was challenging, filled with unexpected twists and turns, but it also brought immense fulfillment and growth. Embracing the unknown opened doors to opportunities and experiences that have enriched my life beyond measure.

Conclusion

Overcoming the fear of the unknown is a transformative process that requires courage, resilience, and a willingness to embrace change. By understanding this fear, recognizing its impact, and employing practical strategies, we can navigate uncharted territories with confidence and grace. Remember, beyond the boundaries of fear lies a world of endless possibilities, waiting to be explored.

As you embark on this journey, take heart in the words of author Joseph Campbell: "The cave you fear to enter holds the treasure you seek." Embrace the unknown, for it is in the unknown that true growth and discovery await.

Chapter 7

CASE STUDIES OF PERSONAL TRANSFORMATION

Introduction
Personal transformation is often the result of profound changes in one's mindset, behaviors, and life circumstances. It is a journey that can be sparked by diverse catalysts, ranging from challenging life events to deliberate self-improvement efforts. This chapter delves into several compelling case studies of individuals who have undergone significant personal transformation, offering insights into the processes, struggles, and triumphs that defined their journeys.

Case Study 1: From Corporate Burnout to Holistic Health Advocate

Background
Meet Rajesh, a high-achieving corporate executive who seemed to have it all—an enviable career, a high salary, and a lifestyle many dream of. However, beneath this facade lay chronic stress, a deteriorating health condition, and a profound sense of dissatisfaction.

Catalyst for Change
The turning point came when Rajesh suffered a severe burnout, resulting in hospitalization. This life-altering event forced him to re-evaluate his priorities and lifestyle choices.

Transformation Process
Rajesh embarked on a holistic journey towards wellness, integrating Ayurveda and mindfulness practices into his daily routine. He resigned from his high-stress job and pursued a certification in holistic health coaching. Through disciplined effort, he transformed his health, mindset, and career.

Outcome
Today, Rajesh is a renowned holistic health advocate, helping others achieve balance and well-being. His story is a testament to the power of

embracing change and prioritizing personal health over professional success.

Case Study 2: The Power of Resilience in the Face of Adversity

Background
Aisha grew up in an underprivileged neighborhood, surrounded by crime and poverty. Despite her circumstances, she had a deep desire for education and a better life.

Catalyst for Change
Tragedy struck when Aisha lost her father at a young age, thrusting her family into deeper financial turmoil. This devastating event, however, fueled her determination to overcome her circumstances.

Transformation Process
Aisha focused intensely on her studies, often studying under streetlights due to lack of electricity at home. She sought out scholarships and mentors who believed in her potential. Through sheer resilience and perseverance, she graduated at the top of her class and earned a full scholarship to a prestigious university.

Outcome
Aisha is now a successful engineer and a community leader, dedicated to empowering other young women from similar backgrounds. Her journey illustrates the power of resilience and the importance of education in personal transformation.

Case Study 3: Rediscovering Purpose through Creative Expression

Background
Sanjay, a mid-level manager in a tech firm, felt stuck in a monotonous job with little fulfillment. Despite financial stability, he experienced a growing sense of purposelessness.

Catalyst for Change

A casual pottery class he attended with friends rekindled a long-lost passion for art and creativity. This seemingly trivial event became a catalyst for significant change.

Transformation Process
Sanjay began dedicating his evenings and weekends to pottery, eventually setting up a small studio at home. The creative process provided him with a new sense of purpose and joy. He started attending art fairs and selling his work, gradually building a side business.

Outcome
Sanjay eventually transitioned to being a full-time artist, leaving his corporate job behind. His case exemplifies how rediscovering and nurturing a passion can lead to profound personal transformation and fulfillment.

Case Study 4: Healing from Trauma and Finding Inner Peace

Background
Priya, a survivor of domestic abuse, struggled with severe PTSD and depression. Her traumatic past left her feeling broken and hopeless.

Catalyst for Change
A recommendation from a friend led Priya to a support group for abuse survivors. The solidarity and shared experiences within this group became the first step in her healing journey.

Transformation Process
Priya engaged in therapy, meditation, and yoga, gradually working through her trauma. She also started writing about her experiences, which served as a therapeutic outlet and helped her connect with others facing similar struggles.

Outcome
Priya has since become a vocal advocate for abuse survivors, sharing her story to inspire and support others. Her transformation from a victim to a survivor and advocate highlights the strength and resilience within individuals to heal and find peace.

Case Study 5: The Journey from Addiction to Recovery

Background
Vikram, once a successful entrepreneur, fell into the throes of addiction following a series of personal and professional failures. His life spiraled out of control, leading to the loss of his business, family, and health.

Catalyst for Change
A near-fatal overdose served as a wake-up call for Vikram. Realizing he was on the brink of losing everything, he decided to seek help.

Transformation Process
Vikram entered a rehabilitation program and committed to a long-term recovery plan. He embraced a 12-step program, engaged in therapy, and found solace in spirituality. He also started volunteering, which gave him a sense of purpose and connection.

Outcome
Today, Vikram is sober and runs a non-profit organization dedicated to helping others overcome addiction. His journey from the depths of addiction to becoming a beacon of hope for others underscores the potential for profound personal transformation through recovery.

Conclusion
These case studies illustrate that personal transformation is often born from adversity and the willingness to embrace change. Each story highlights different pathways to growth, emphasizing the importance of resilience, passion, support systems, and purposeful action. Through these narratives, we see that transformation is not just possible but attainable for anyone willing to embark on the journey beyond their boundaries.

Chapter 8

SELF-DISCOVERY AND AWARENESS

Introduction

Self-discovery and awareness form the foundation of personal growth. Understanding who we are, what we value, and what drives us is essential for living a fulfilling life. This chapter explores the journey of self-discovery, the importance of self-awareness, and practical steps to deepen our understanding of ourselves.

The Journey of Self-Discovery

Self-discovery is a lifelong journey. It involves exploring our inner world, uncovering our passions, and identifying our strengths and weaknesses. This process requires courage, honesty, and an open mind. Here are some steps to embark on this journey:

Reflect on Your Past: Our past experiences shape that we are today. Reflecting on these experiences can provide insights into our values, beliefs, and behaviors. Consider the pivotal moments in your life and how they have influenced you.

Identify Your Values: Values are the principles that guide our decisions and actions. Knowing what we value helps us make choices that align with our true selves. Take time to identify your core values and consider how they influence your life.

Explore Your Passions: Passion drives us to pursue our goals and dreams. Identifying what excites and motivates us can lead to a more fulfilling life. Reflect on the activities that bring you joy and fulfillment.

Understand Your Strengths and Weaknesses: Acknowledging our strengths and weaknesses allows us to leverage our abilities and address areas for improvement. Seek feedback from others and engage in self-assessment to gain a clearer picture of your capabilities.

The Importance of Self-Awareness

Self-awareness is the ability to recognize and understand our emotions, thoughts, and behaviors. It is crucial for personal growth as it helps us:

Make Informed Decisions: Self-awareness allows us to make decisions that align with our values and goals. By understanding our motivations and triggers, we can choose actions that are true to ourselves.

Improve Relationships: Understanding our emotions and how they impact our interactions with others can lead to healthier and more meaningful relationships. Self-awareness fosters empathy and effective communication.

Enhance Emotional Intelligence: Emotional intelligence involves recognizing and managing our emotions and those of others. Self-awareness is the first step in developing this skill, which is essential for personal and professional success.

Foster Personal Growth: Being aware of our strengths and areas for improvement enables us to set realistic goals and work towards them. Self-awareness is the foundation of continuous self-improvement.

Practical Steps to Deepen Self-Awareness

Practice Mindfulness: Mindfulness involves paying attention to the present moment without judgment. It helps us become more aware of our thoughts and feelings. Practice mindfulness through meditation, deep breathing, or simply observing your surroundings.

Journal Regularly: Writing about your thoughts and experiences can provide insights into your inner world. Journaling helps clarify your emotions and track your personal growth over time.

Seek Feedback: Others can offer valuable perspectives on our behavior and actions. Ask for feedback from trusted friends, family, or colleagues and reflect on their observations.

Engage in Self-Reflection: Set aside time regularly to reflect on your day, your decisions, and your interactions with others. Consider what you learned and how you can apply these insights moving forward.

Set Personal Goals: Setting and achieving personal goals can increase self-awareness. Goals provide direction and motivation, helping us understand what we truly want and value.

Embracing the Journey

Self-discovery and awareness are ongoing processes that require patience and dedication. Embrace the journey with an open heart and mind, and be gentle with yourself as you uncover the layers of your true self. Remember, personal growth is not about perfection but about progress and understanding.

As you continue on this path, you will find greater clarity, purpose, and fulfillment in all aspects of your life. The journey of self-discovery and awareness is a powerful step towards living beyond boundaries, allowing you to reach your full potential and lead a more meaningful and authentic life.

In this chapter, we explored the significance of self-discovery and awareness, practical steps to enhance our understanding of ourselves, and the importance of embracing this lifelong journey. As you move forward in this book, continue to apply these principles to achieve personal growth and live a life that truly reflects who you are.

Chapter 9

TOOLS AND TECHNIQUES FOR SELF-DISCOVERY

Introduction

Self-discovery is a profound journey that requires deep introspection and a willingness to explore the layers of our identity. It involves understanding our passions, values, strengths, and weaknesses. This chapter delves into the essential tools and techniques that can guide you on this transformative path of self-discovery.

1. Journaling

Journaling is a powerful tool for self-reflection and personal growth. It provides a safe space to express thoughts and emotions, helping you gain clarity and insight into your inner world.

Techniques

Daily Reflection: Spend a few minutes each day writing about your experiences, feelings, and thoughts. This practice can reveal patterns in your behavior and emotions.

Prompt-Based Writing: Use prompts like "What am I grateful for today?" or "What challenges did I face today?" to explore specific aspects of your life.

Stream of Consciousness: Write continuously without worrying about grammar or structure. This free-flowing method can uncover subconscious thoughts and feelings.

2. Meditation and Mindfulness

Meditation and mindfulness practices help you become more aware of your thoughts and emotions, fostering a deeper connection with your true self.

Techniques

Breathe Awareness: Focus on your breath to anchor your mind in the present moment, reducing stress and enhancing self-awareness.

Body Scan: Pay attention to each part of your body, noticing sensations without judgment. This practice can help you understand how emotions manifest physically.

Guided Meditation: Use apps or recordings to follow guided meditations that lead you through visualization exercises and self-reflective prompts.

3. Personality Assessments

Personality assessments can provide valuable insights into your character traits, preferences, and tendencies.

Popular Assessments

Myers-Briggs Type Indicator (MBTI): Identifies your personality type based on preferences in how you perceive the world and make decisions.

Enneagram: Explores nine different personality types, highlighting core motivations, fears, and growth opportunities.

Strengths Finder: Identifies your top strengths, helping you leverage them for personal and professional development.

4. Creative Expression

Engaging in creative activities can unlock hidden aspects of your personality and provide a deeper understanding of your inner self.

Techniques

Art Therapy: Use drawing, painting, or sculpting to express your emotions and explore your subconscious mind.

Writing: Write poetry, fiction, or personal essays to articulate your thoughts and feelings.

Music and Dance: Use music and movement to connect with your emotions and release stress.

5. Coaching and Therapy

Working with a coach or therapist can provide personalized guidance and support on your self-discovery journey.

Approaches

Life Coaching: Focuses on setting and achieving personal goals, providing tools and strategies for growth.

Psychotherapy: Addresses deeper emotional and psychological issues, helping you understand and overcome past traumas and limiting beliefs. Group Therapy: Offers a supportive environment to share experiences and learn from others on similar journeys.

6. Self-Reflection Exercises

Self-reflection exercises encourage you to examine your thoughts, behaviors, and experiences to gain insight into your true self.

Techniques

SWOT Analysis: Identify your Strengths, Weaknesses, Opportunities, and Threats to understand your current position and potential growth areas.

Wheel of Life: Evaluate different areas of your life (e.g., career, relationships, health) to identify imbalances and areas for improvement.

Vision Board: Create a visual representation of your goals and aspirations to clarify your desires and motivations.

7. Nature and Solitude

Spending time in nature and embracing solitude like the great scientist Einstein can help you reconnect with your inner self and gain clarity on your life's purpose.

Techniques

Nature Walks: Take regular walks in natural settings to clear your mind and reflect on your thoughts.

Solo Retreats: Spend time alone in a quiet, peaceful environment to disconnect from distractions and focus on self-reflection.

Gardening: Engage in gardening to cultivate patience, mindfulness, and a deeper connection with the natural world.

Conclusion

Self-discovery is an ongoing journey that requires dedication, patience, and an open mind. By utilizing these tools and techniques, you can uncover the depths of your true self and embark on a path of personal growth and fulfillment. Embrace the process, and remember that each step you take brings you closer to understanding your authentic self.

Chapter 10

THE ROLE OF MINDFULNESS

In the journey of personal growth, the practice of mindfulness stands out as a fundamental cornerstone. Mindfulness, often defined as the quality of being present and fully engaged with the current moment, holds transformative potential in our lives. By fostering a deeper awareness of our thoughts, emotions, and sensations, mindfulness allows us to navigate life's challenges with greater clarity and compassion.

Understanding Mindfulness

Mindfulness originates from ancient meditation practices, particularly within Buddhist traditions. However, its benefits have transcended cultural and religious boundaries, gaining recognition in contemporary psychology and healthcare. At its core, mindfulness is about paying attention in a particular way: on purpose, in the present moment, and non-judgmentally.

Jon Kabat-Zinn, a pioneer in the field of mindfulness-based stress reduction (MBSR), emphasizes that mindfulness is not about eliminating thoughts or achieving a state of perpetual calm. Instead, it is about cultivating an attitude of openness and curiosity toward our experiences, allowing us to respond to situations with greater wisdom and patience.

The Benefits of Mindfulness

Emotional Regulation: Mindfulness helps us become more aware of our emotions and the triggers behind them. By observing our feelings without immediate reaction, we gain the space to choose our responses rather than being driven by automatic patterns. This leads to better emotional regulation and reduced reactivity.

Stress Reduction: Numerous studies have shown that mindfulness practices can significantly reduce stress. By focusing on the present moment, we break the cycle of rumination and worry that often fuels anxiety. Mindfulness encourages a state of relaxation and helps lower cortisol levels, the body's primary stress hormone.

Enhanced Focus and Concentration: In our fast-paced world, distractions are rampant. Mindfulness trains the mind to sustain attention on a single task, improving our ability to concentrate and enhancing productivity. This is particularly valuable in both personal and professional settings.

Improved Relationships: Mindfulness fosters empathy and active listening, which are crucial for healthy relationships. By being fully present with others, we communicate more effectively and build deeper connections. This practice also helps us manage conflicts with greater calm and understanding.

Increased Self-Awareness: Through mindfulness, we develop a clearer understanding of our thoughts, behaviors, and motivations. This heightened self-awareness is the first step toward personal growth, enabling us to make conscious choices aligned with our values and goals.

Integrating Mindfulness into Daily Life

Incorporating mindfulness into our daily routine does not require extensive time or effort. Here are some practical ways to integrate mindfulness into everyday activities:

Mindful Breathing: Take a few moments each day to focus on your breath. Pay attention to the sensation of the air entering and leaving your nostrils. This simple practice can anchor you in the present moment and bring a sense of calm.

Mindful Eating: During meals, take the time to savor each bite. Notice the flavors, textures, and aromas of your food. Eating mindfully enhances the dining experience and promotes better digestion.

Mindful Walking: Whether you're walking in a park or just down the hallway, bring your awareness to the act of walking. Feel the ground beneath your feet and the rhythm of your steps. This practice can transform a mundane activity into a meditative experience.

Mindful Listening: When interacting with others, give them your full attention. Listen without planning your response or getting distracted by your thoughts. This not only improves communication but also strengthens your relationships.

Body Scan: Set aside a few minutes each day to mentally scan your body from head to toe. Notice any areas of tension or discomfort and breathe into them. This practice promotes relaxation and body awareness.

Overcoming Challenges in Mindfulness Practice

While the benefits of mindfulness are well-documented, many people face challenges in maintaining a consistent practice. Common obstacles include a busy schedule, restlessness, and unrealistic expectations. Here are some tips to overcome these challenges:

Start Small: Begin with short sessions of mindfulness practice, such as five minutes a day, and gradually increase the duration as you become more comfortable.

Create a Routine: Incorporate mindfulness into your daily routine by linking it to an existing habit, such as brushing your teeth or drinking your morning coffee. This makes it easier to remember and practice regularly.

Be Patient: Mindfulness is a skill that develops over time. Be patient with yourself and let go of any expectations of immediate results. The benefits will accrue with consistent practice.

Seek Support: Consider joining a mindfulness group or attending a workshop. Sharing your experiences with others can provide motivation and enhance your understanding of the practice.

The Transformative Power of Mindfulness

Mindfulness is not a panacea, but it is a powerful tool for personal growth. By cultivating mindfulness, we learn to live more fully in the present moment, manage our emotions more effectively, and build deeper connections with ourselves and others. This practice nurtures a sense of inner peace and resilience, enabling us to navigate life's challenges with grace and wisdom.

In embracing mindfulness, we embark on a journey of self-discovery and transformation. As we become more attuned to our inner experiences, we unlock the potential for profound personal growth. The role of mindfulness in our lives is not just about reducing stress or improving focus; it is about fostering a deeper connection with ourselves and the world around us. Through mindfulness, we truly begin to live beyond boundaries.

Chapter 11

STORIES OF INDIVIDUALS WHO FOUND THEIR TRUE SELVES

Finding one's true self is often a journey marked by challenges, self-discovery, and transformation. In this chapter, we delve into inspiring stories of individuals who embarked on this journey, faced their inner conflicts, and emerged as their authentic selves. These narratives demonstrate that the path to self-discovery is not linear but filled with meaningful experiences that shape and redefine who we are.

1. The Rebirth of Maya: From Corporate Climb to Creative Freedom

Maya was a high-powered executive at a leading multinational corporation. For years, she thrived on the fast pace and the prestige that came with her role. However, despite her success, Maya felt an inexplicable void. Her life was a series of meetings, presentations, and targets, leaving little room for personal fulfillment.

One day, during a rare vacation, Maya attended a pottery workshop. As her hands molded the clay, she felt an unexpected sense of peace and joy. This simple act ignited a long-suppressed passion for art. Encouraged by the experience, Maya began spending her weekends in art studios, reconnecting with her creative side. Over time, she realized that her true self was not confined to the corporate ladder but expressed through her artistry.

With courage and conviction, Maya decided to leave her job and pursue a career as an artist. The transition was challenging, but she found immense satisfaction in creating art that resonated with her soul. Today, Maya is a renowned artist whose works are celebrated globally. Her journey from the corporate world to creative freedom exemplifies how following one's passion can lead to discovering one's true self.

2. Alex's Journey: From Self-Doubt to Self-Acceptance

Alex grew up in a conservative family where academic excellence was highly valued. As a child, he excelled in his studies, but deep down, he struggled with his identity. Alex knew he was different but feared rejection from his family and society.

In college, Alex met people from diverse backgrounds and slowly started to accept his true identity. He joined a support group for LGBTQ+ individuals, where he found a community that embraced him for who he was. The support and acceptance he received gave him the strength to come out to his family.

Although the initial reaction was difficult, over time, his family began to understand and accept him. Alex's journey from self-doubt to self-acceptance was not easy, but it was liberating. Today, he is an advocate for LGBTQ+ rights, working to create a world where everyone can live authentically without fear of judgment. Alex's story is a testament to the power of self-acceptance and the importance of living one's truth.

3. Sara's Transformation: From Burnout to Balanced Life

Sara was a dedicated nurse who loved her job but often found herself overwhelmed by the demands of her profession. The long hours and emotional toll led to burnout, and she realized that she had lost sight of who she was outside of her role as a caregiver.

Determined to reclaim her life, Sara took a sabbatical and embarked on a journey of self-discovery. She traveled, practiced mindfulness, and explored hobbies she had long neglected. Through this process, Sara learned the importance of balance and self-care. She discovered a passion for yoga and became a certified instructor.

Upon returning to her profession, Sara implemented new routines that allowed her to maintain a healthy work-life balance. She also started a wellness program for her colleagues, promoting the importance of self-care in the healthcare industry. Sara's transformation from burnout to a balanced life illustrates that finding one's true self often involves creating harmony between personal and professional life.

4. Rahul's Realization: From Wealth to Wisdom

Rahul was a successful entrepreneur who had amassed considerable wealth. Despite his financial success, he felt a profound emptiness. The relentless pursuit of money and status left him questioning the true meaning of life.

Seeking answers, Rahul decided to take a break from his business and travel to a remote village in India. There, he lived a simple life, volunteering at a local school and connecting with the villagers. Through their stories and experiences, he learned valuable lessons about contentment, community, and the essence of happiness.

Rahul returned with a renewed perspective. He shifted his business focus to social entrepreneurship, aiming to create positive change in society. His journey from wealth to wisdom taught him that true fulfillment comes not from external achievements but from inner growth and contributing to the greater good.

5.   Ana's Awakening: From Perfectionism to Purpose

Ana was a perfectionist who strived for excellence in everything she did. Her need for perfection often left she stressed and dissatisfied, as she constantly felt she wasn't good enough. This mindset took a toll on her mental health, and she realized she needed a change.

Ana started attending personal development workshops and practicing self-compassion. She learned to embrace her imperfections and focus on her strengths. This shift in perspective allowed her to discover her true purpose: helping others overcome perfectionism and embrace their authentic selves.

Ana became a life coach, using her experiences to guide others on their journey to self-discovery. Her story highlights the importance of letting go of unrealistic standards and finding purpose in helping others navigate similar challenges.

Conclusion

These stories of Maya, Alex, Sara, Rahul, and Ana remind us that the journey to finding our true selves is unique for each individual. It requires courage, self-reflection, and a willingness to embrace change. Whether through creative expression, self-acceptance, balance, wisdom, or purpose, these individuals found their true selves by breaking free from societal expectations and following their inner voice. Their journeys inspire us to embark on our own path of self-discovery, encouraging us to live authentically and beyond boundaries.

Chapter 12

UNDERSTANDING AND BUILDING RESILIENCE

Resilience is the capacity to bounce back from adversity, challenges, and setbacks. It's a crucial quality that enables individuals to navigate life's ups and downs with grace and strength. Building resilience involves developing a set of skills and attitudes that empower you to face difficulties head-on, learn from them, and emerge stronger. This chapter explores the components of resilience, strategies to cultivate it, and the profound impact it can have on your personal growth journey.

Understanding Resilience

Resilience is not an inherent trait that some people possess while others do not. Rather, it is a dynamic process that anyone can develop and strengthen. It involves a combination of emotional, cognitive, and behavioral skills that help you cope with stress and adversity. At its core, resilience is about maintaining a positive outlook, adapting to change, and persevering through challenges.

The Components of Resilience

Self-Awareness: Understanding your emotions, strengths, weaknesses, and triggers is the foundation of resilience. Self-awareness allows you to recognize when you're feeling overwhelmed and take proactive steps to manage your emotions.

Optimism: Maintaining a positive outlook, even in difficult situations, is crucial for resilience. Optimism doesn't mean ignoring reality but rather focusing on the possibilities and solutions.

Emotional Regulation: The ability to manage your emotions in stressful situations helps prevent them from becoming overwhelming. Techniques such as deep breathing, mindfulness, and meditation can aid in emotional regulation.

Self-Efficacy: Believing in your ability to influence events and outcomes is essential for resilience. Developing self-efficacy involves setting realistic goals, celebrating small victories, and learning from failures.

Social Support: Building and maintaining strong relationships provides a network of support during tough times. Sharing your experiences and seeking advice from trusted friends and family can offer new perspectives and comfort.

Problem-Solving Skills: Effective problem-solving skills enable you to tackle challenges systematically and find workable solutions. This involves breaking problems down into manageable parts and considering multiple options.

Adaptability: Being flexible and open to change helps you adjust to new circumstances. Embracing change as an opportunity for growth rather than a threat fosters resilience.

Purpose and Meaning: Having a sense of purpose and meaning in life provides motivation and direction. Pursuing goals that align with your values and passions can sustain you through difficult times.

Strategies for Building Resilience

Develop a Growth Mindset: Embrace challenges as opportunities to learn and grow. Viewing setbacks as temporary and surmountable helps you maintain motivation and perseverance.

Practice Mindfulness: Mindfulness practices, such as meditation and deep breathing, help you stay present and reduce stress. Regular mindfulness practice can enhance your emotional regulation and self-awareness.

Build Strong Relationships: Cultivate a network of supportive relationships. Invest time in building and maintaining connections with family, friends, and colleagues. Don't hesitate to seek support when needed.

Set Realistic Goals: Break down larger goals into smaller, achievable steps. Celebrate your progress and use setbacks as learning experiences. This approach helps build self-efficacy and keeps you motivated.

Maintain Physical Health: Regular exercise, a balanced diet, and adequate sleep are crucial for physical and mental well-being. Physical health directly impacts your ability to cope with stress.

Practice Gratitude: Regularly reflecting on things you're grateful for can shift your focus from what's wrong to what's right in your life. Gratitude practices have been shown to enhance well-being and resilience.

Seek Professional Help: If you're struggling to cope with stress or adversity, consider seeking help from a mental health professional. Therapy or counseling can provide valuable tools and support for building resilience.

The Impact of Resilience on Personal Growth

Building resilience transforms the way you approach life. It empowers you to face challenges with confidence, adapt to change, and maintain a positive outlook. Resilience fosters personal growth by helping you:

Develop Greater Self-Confidence: Overcoming challenges and learning from failures boosts your self-efficacy and confidence in your abilities.

Enhance Emotional Intelligence: Managing emotions effectively and maintaining healthy relationships contribute to higher emotional intelligence.

Cultivate a Positive Outlook: Resilience helps you focus on possibilities and solutions rather than dwelling on problems. This positive mindset enhances your overall well-being.

Strengthen Problem-Solving Skills: Regularly facing and overcoming challenges sharpens your problem-solving abilities, making you more adept at navigating future obstacles.

Foster Adaptability: Embracing change and viewing it as an opportunity for growth helps you remain flexible and open-minded.

Conclusion

Building resilience is an ongoing journey that involves developing a set of skills and attitudes to navigate life's challenges effectively. By cultivating self-awareness, optimism, emotional regulation, self-efficacy, social support, problem-solving skills, adaptability, and a sense of purpose, you can enhance your resilience and achieve personal growth. Resilience not only helps you bounce back from adversity but also empowers you to thrive in the face of change, ultimately leading to a more fulfilling and meaningful life.

Chapter 13

INSPIRING ANECDOTES OF RESILIENT INDIVIDUALS

Introduction

Resilience is the remarkable ability to bounce back from adversity, adapt to change, and emerge stronger. It is a trait that distinguishes individuals who not only survive but thrive despite the challenges they face. In this chapter, we explore inspiring anecdotes of resilient individuals who have transcended boundaries through their courage, determination, and unwavering spirit.

1. Helen Keller: Overcoming the Darkness

Helen Keller's story is a profound testament to resilience. Born in 1880, Keller lost her sight and hearing at just 19 months old due to an illness. Despite these severe disabilities, Keller's spirit remained unbroken. With the relentless support of her teacher, Anne Sullivan, she learned to communicate through the manual alphabet and eventually graduated from Radcliffe College with honors.

Keller's life was a journey of breaking barriers. She became a world-renowned author, activist, and lecturer. Her resilience was not merely about overcoming her disabilities but also about her relentless fight for social justice and equality. Keller's story teaches us that even the most formidable obstacles can be overcome with perseverance and support.

2. Nelson Mandela: The Power of Forgiveness

Nelson Mandela's life exemplifies the transformative power of resilience. Imprisoned for 27 years for his anti-apartheid activities, Mandela faced harsh conditions and the constant threat of despair. However, his resilience was not rooted in bitterness but in hope and forgiveness.

Upon his release in 1990, Mandela did not seek revenge but worked towards reconciliation. His leadership helped dismantle apartheid and establish a multiracial democracy in South Africa. Mandela's resilience lay in his ability to endure suffering with grace and use his experience to heal a nation. His story illustrates how resilience can turn personal suffering into a force for societal change.

3. Malala Yousafzai: A Voice for Education

Malala Yousafzai's story is a powerful example of youthful resilience. In 2012, at just 15 years old, Malala was shot by the Taliban for advocating girls' education in Pakistan. The attack was a brutal attempt to silence her, but it only amplified her voice.

After surviving the assassination attempt, Malala continued her advocacy with even greater determination. She became the youngest-ever Nobel Prize laureate in 2014. Her resilience is evident in her unwavering commitment to education and her ability to turn a violent attack into a global movement for girls' rights. Malala's journey teaches us that resilience can transform personal adversity into a platform for global impact.

4. J.K. Rowling: From Struggles to Success

Before becoming a household name, J.K. Rowling faced significant personal and professional struggles. She was a single mother living on welfare, battling depression, and facing numerous rejections from publishers. Despite these obstacles, Rowling remained resolute in her dream of becoming a writer.

Her perseverance paid off with the publication of the first Harry Potter book, which eventually became a global phenomenon. Rowling's resilience was reflected in her ability to overcome her circumstances and continue pursuing her passion despite repeated setbacks. Her story is a testament to how determination and persistence can lead to extraordinary success.

5. Stephen Hawking: Defying the Odds

Stephen Hawking's life is a remarkable example of resilience in the face of debilitating illness. Diagnosed with amyotrophic lateral sclerosis (ALS) at age 21 and given a short time to live, Hawking defied medical expectations by living for over four decades. His condition gradually paralyzed him, but his mind remained incredibly sharp.

Hawking continued to make groundbreaking contributions to theoretical physics, including his work on black holes and cosmology. His resilience was characterized by his ability to focus on his intellectual pursuits and maintain a sense of humor despite his physical limitations. Hawking's story demonstrates that resilience involves not just enduring hardship but also thriving intellectually and creatively.

6. Dr. A.P.J. Abdul Kalam: The People's President

Dr. A.P.J. Abdul Kalam, widely known as the "People's President" of India, was an embodiment of resilience and vision. Born in 1931 in a small village in Tamil Nadu, Kalam's early life was marked by poverty and humble beginnings. His father, a boat owner, and his mother, a homemaker, instilled in him the values of hard work and humility.

Despite financial constraints, Kalam was determined to pursue his education. He studied aerospace engineering at the Madras Institute of Technology, overcoming numerous obstacles along the way. His resilience was evident in his unwavering commitment to his studies and his eventual success in the field of aerospace engineering.

Kalam's career took a significant turn when he joined the Indian Space Research Organisation (ISRO). During his tenure, he played a crucial role in India's first satellite launch, Aryabhata, and the development of the Indian missile program. His work faced many challenges, including technical failures and skepticism from various quarters. Yet, Kalam remained steadfast, leading to the successful development of indigenous missiles and placing India on the global aerospace map.

His resilience was not confined to his professional life. After serving as the President of India from 2002 to 2007, Kalam continued to inspire and educate young minds through his lectures and writings. His book, "Wings of Fire," is a testament to his life's journey and his belief in the power of dreams and perseverance.

Dr. Kalam's story teaches us that resilience is not merely about enduring hardships but also about using those experiences to fuel one's passion and achieve greatness. His life reminds us that with determination and a clear vision, we can overcome any obstacle and leave a lasting impact on the world.

7. Baba Amte: The Mahatma of Social Work

Baba Amte, born Murlidhar Devidas Amte in 1914, was a revered social activist and philanthropist known for his work with leprosy patients and marginalized communities. His journey from a well-to-do lawyer to a dedicated social worker is a powerful example of resilience and compassion.

Amte's life took a transformative turn when he decided to leave his successful legal career to work with leprosy patients. In the 1950s, leprosy was a highly stigmatized disease, and those afflicted were often shunned by society. Undeterred by societal prejudices and personal risk, Amte founded the Anandwan community in Maharashtra, a sanctuary for leprosy patients and their families.

The challenges he faced were immense. The Anandwan community struggled with limited resources, societal resistance, and the physical and emotional toll of working with individuals suffering from a debilitating disease. However, Amte's resilience shone through as he tirelessly worked to provide medical care, education, and rehabilitation for his patients. His efforts transformed Anandwan into a self-sustaining community where individuals with leprosy could lead dignified and productive lives.

Amte's resilience extended beyond his work with leprosy patients. He was deeply committed to social justice, advocating for the rights of the marginalized and championing various social causes. His work earned him numerous accolades, including the Padma Bhushan and the Ramon Magsaysay Award.

Baba Amte's life story is a powerful reminder that resilience is often about confronting societal norms and personal challenges with unwavering determination and compassion. His legacy continues to inspire those who seek to make a difference in the world, demonstrating that even in the face of adversity, one person's dedication and resilience can effect profound change.

Conclusion

These stories illustrate the diverse ways in which resilience can manifest. Their experiences remind us that resilience is not a passive trait but an active process of overcoming, adapting, and growing. As we reflect on their journeys, we find that resilience is a powerful tool for transcending personal and collective boundaries, enabling us to face challenges with courage and emerge stronger.

Incorporating these examples into our own lives can inspire us to harness our inner strength, overcome our adversities, and achieve personal growth beyond boundaries.

PART II
Professional Excellence beyond Boundaries

Chapter 14

INNOVATION AND CREATIVITY

Introduction

Innovation and creativity are the lifeblood of professional excellence. In a rapidly evolving world, where change is constant and competition is fierce, the ability to think creatively and innovate is what sets leaders and organizations apart. This chapter explores the essence of innovation and creativity, how they intersect, and practical strategies to harness them for professional growth and success.

The Essence of Innovation and Creativity

At its core, creativity is about generating novel ideas and approaches. It's the capacity to think outside conventional frameworks and envision possibilities that others might overlook. Innovation, on the other hand, involves the practical application of these creative ideas to solve problems, improve processes, or create new value. While creativity is the spark that ignites the fire, innovation is the fuel that sustains it.

The Role of Creativity in Professional Success

Creativity is not confined to artistic endeavors. In the professional realm, it is equally crucial. Creative problem-solving enables individuals and organizations to tackle challenges in unique ways, often leading to groundbreaking solutions. For example, tech giants like Apple and Google have thrived by fostering creative environments that encourage unconventional thinking.

To cultivate creativity in your professional life, consider the following strategies:

Encourage Curiosity: Embrace a mindset of continuous learning. Explore new fields, read widely, and seek out diverse perspectives.

Foster a Creative Environment: Create spaces that stimulate creativity. This might include flexible workspaces, access to diverse resources, or regular brainstorming sessions.

Embrace Failure: View failures as learning opportunities. Encourage experimentation and be open to iterative processes that refine ideas over time.

Innovation: Turning Ideas into Reality

While creativity generates ideas, innovation is about bringing those ideas to fruition. It involves strategic planning, resource allocation, and execution. Successful innovation requires a systematic approach:

Identify Opportunities: Look for gaps in the market, inefficiencies, or emerging trends that align with your organization's goals.

Develop a Strategy: Formulate a clear plan that outlines how your innovative idea will be implemented. This includes setting objectives, defining key performance indicators, and allocating resources.

Execute and Evaluate: Implement your strategy and continuously monitor its progress. Use feedback to make adjustments and improvements.

Case Studies in Innovation

Examining real-world examples can provide valuable insights into how innovation works in practice. Consider the case of Netflix. Initially a DVD rental service, Netflix innovated by shifting to a streaming model, thereby revolutionizing the entertainment industry. Their success can be attributed to their ability to anticipate market trends, invest in technology, and adapt their business model.

Another example is Tesla. By pushing the boundaries of electric vehicle technology and renewable energy, Tesla has redefined the automotive industry. Their innovation stems from a commitment to research and development, bold vision, and a willingness to challenge the status quo.

Cultivating a Culture of Innovation

For innovation to thrive, it must be embedded in the organizational culture. Here are some ways to cultivate such a culture

Encourage Collaboration: Promote cross-functional teamwork to bring diverse perspectives to problem-solving.

Recognize and Reward Innovation: Celebrate successes and acknowledge contributions that drive innovation.

Provide Resources: Invest in tools, technologies, and training that support innovative thinking and experimentation.

Conclusion

Innovation and creativity are not just buzzwords; they are critical components of professional excellence. By nurturing your creative abilities and adopting strategies to turn ideas into impactful innovations, you can position yourself and your organization at the forefront of progress. As the world continues to change, those who embrace and excel in these areas will lead the way in shaping the future of their industries.

This chapter aims to provide a comprehensive understanding of how to harness innovation and creativity for professional excellence. By integrating these principles into your career, you can overcome boundaries and achieve remarkable success.

Chapter 15

FOSTERING A CULTURE OF INNOVATION

Introduction

In today's rapidly evolving world, fostering a culture of innovation is crucial for any organization aspiring to maintain a competitive edge and achieve long-term success. Innovation is not just about developing new products or services; it encompasses a broader mindset that encourages continuous improvement, creative problem-solving, and a willingness to challenge the status quo. This chapter explores strategies to cultivate an environment where innovation thrives, examining the principles, practices, and leadership approaches that drive a culture of innovation.

Understanding Innovation

Innovation can be defined as the process of translating new ideas into tangible outcomes that provide value. It involves not just invention but also the application of creative solutions to address challenges and seize opportunities. There are several types of innovation, including:

Product Innovation: Developing new or improved products.

Process Innovation: Enhancing existing processes to increase efficiency and effectiveness.

Business Model Innovation: Redefining how an organization creates, delivers, and captures value.

Service Innovation: Introducing new or enhanced services to meet customer needs.

The Importance of a Culture of Innovation

A culture of innovation drives organizational growth and adaptability. It empowers employees to think creatively and contribute ideas, fostering an environment where experimentation and learning are encouraged. Key benefits include:

Enhanced Problem-Solving: Innovative cultures generate diverse ideas, leading to more effective solutions to complex problems.

Competitive Advantage: Organizations that innovate can differentiate themselves in the market, attracting customers and gaining a competitive edge.

Employee Engagement: When employees feel their ideas are valued, they are more engaged and motivated, contributing to higher job satisfaction and retention.

Creating an Environment that Fosters Innovation

Encourage Open Communication: Promote an open and transparent communication environment where ideas can be freely shared. Encourage team members to voice their opinions and provide constructive feedback.

Embrace Risk-Taking: Innovation often involves taking risks. Encourage a mindset that views failure as a learning opportunity rather than a setback. Celebrate both successes and lessons learned from failures.

Provide Resources and Support: Allocate resources, including time, funding, and training, to support innovation initiatives. Provide employees with the tools and support they need to experiment and implement new ideas.

Foster Collaboration: Create opportunities for cross-functional collaboration. Diverse teams with varying perspectives can generate more innovative solutions than isolated groups.

Lead by Example: Leadership plays a crucial role in shaping the culture of innovation. Leaders should model innovative behavior, demonstrate a commitment to continuous improvement, and support their teams in pursuing innovative projects.

Recognize and Reward Innovation: Acknowledge and reward employees who contribute innovative ideas and solutions. Recognition can take various forms, such as awards, bonuses, or public acknowledgment, reinforcing the value of innovation within the organization.

Promote Continuous Learning: Encourage a culture of continuous learning and development. Provide opportunities for employees to expand their skills and knowledge, stay informed about industry trends, and explore new technologies.

Implement a Structured Innovation Process: Develop a structured process for managing innovation, including idea generation, evaluation, and implementation. This ensures that innovative ideas are systematically explored and developed.

Overcoming Barriers to Innovation

While fostering a culture of innovation is essential, organizations may encounter barriers that hinder progress. Common challenges include:

Resistance to Change: Employees may resist new ideas or changes to established processes. Overcome resistance by involving employees in the change process and addressing their concerns.

Lack of Resources: Limited resources can constrain innovation efforts. Prioritize innovation initiatives and seek external support if necessary.

Fear of Failure: Fear of failure can stifle creativity. Cultivate a culture where failure is seen as a stepping stone to success and provide support for risk-taking.

Conclusion

Fostering a culture of innovation requires deliberate effort and commitment from all levels of an organization. By creating an environment that encourages creativity, embraces risk, and supports continuous learning, organizations can drive growth, enhance problem-solving, and achieve a competitive advantage. Leaders play a pivotal role in shaping this culture, and their commitment to innovation will inspire and motivate their teams to think beyond boundaries and drive meaningful change.

As we move forward in a world that values innovation, embracing these principles and practices will empower organizations to navigate challenges, seize opportunities, and thrive in an ever-evolving landscape.

Chapter 16

THE INTERSECTION OF CREATIVITY AND PROFESSIONAL SUCCESS

Introduction

In today's rapidly evolving professional landscape, creativity is not merely a desirable trait but a critical component of success. The ability to innovate, adapt, and think outside the box distinguishes leading professionals from their peers. This chapter explores how creativity intersects with professional success, offering insights into harnessing creative potential for career advancement and organizational growth.

Understanding Creativity in a Professional Context

Creativity in the professional world involves more than artistic expression; it encompasses problem-solving, strategic thinking, and the ability to envision new possibilities. It is the capacity to generate original ideas, connect disparate concepts, and apply innovative solutions to challenges. Creative professionals often excel in roles that require adaptability, strategic planning, and complex problem resolution.

The Role of Creativity in Professional Success

Innovation and Problem Solving: Creativity drives innovation, which is crucial for organizational growth. Companies that foster a creative environment are better positioned to develop new products, services, and processes. Creative problem solving also enables professionals to navigate complex challenges and find unique solutions, setting them apart in competitive fields.

Adaptability and Resilience: In a world where change is constant, creativity aids in adaptability. Professionals who embrace creative thinking are more resilient and open to new approaches, making them better equipped to handle shifts in industry trends, technological advancements, and market demands.

Leadership and Vision: Creative leaders inspire and motivate their teams by envisioning future possibilities and articulating a compelling vision. They encourage innovation and foster a culture of creativity within their organizations, leading to enhanced team performance and organizational success.

Personal Branding and Career Advancement: Creativity can significantly impact personal branding. Professionals who showcase their innovative thinking and problem-solving abilities stand out to employers and clients. By demonstrating a unique approach and delivering creative solutions, individuals enhance their professional reputation and career prospects.

Cultivating Creativity for Professional Growth

Encouraging a Creative Mindset: Developing a creative mindset involves cultivating curiosity, openness to new experiences, and a willingness to take risks. Embrace challenges as opportunities for growth and view failures as learning experiences rather than setbacks.

Diverse Experiences and Learning: Exposure to diverse experiences and knowledge broadens perspectives and fuels creativity. Engage in activities outside your primary field of expertise, such as attending workshops, pursuing hobbies, or collaborating with individuals from different backgrounds.

Creating a Supportive Environment: Work environments that support creativity foster collaboration, experimentation, and risk-taking. Encourage open communication, provide resources for creative projects, and recognize and reward innovative contributions.

Time for Reflection and Ideation: Allocate time for reflection and ideation. Creative insights often emerge during periods of contemplation, so incorporating regular brainstorming sessions and setting aside time for uninterrupted thought can enhance creative output.

Case Studies and Examples

Steve Jobs and Apple: Steve Jobs exemplified the intersection of creativity and professional success. His visionary approach and emphasis on design and user experience transformed Apple into a leader in technology and innovation.

IDEO and Design Thinking: The design firm IDEO revolutionized product development through its creative approach known as design thinking. By focusing on empathy and user-centered design, IDEO created groundbreaking solutions across various industries.

Conclusion

The intersection of creativity and professional success is a dynamic and powerful nexus. Creativity not only drives innovation and problem-solving but also enhances adaptability, leadership, and personal branding. By nurturing creative skills and fostering an environment that values innovation, professionals can achieve significant success and make meaningful contributions to their fields. Embrace creativity as a cornerstone of professional excellence and unlock new possibilities for growth and achievement.

This chapter provides a comprehensive overview of how creativity intersects with professional success, offering practical advice and real-world examples to illustrate its importance.

Chapter 17

EXAMPLES OF INNOVATIVE THINKERS

Introduction

In a rapidly evolving world, professional excellence often hinges on the ability to think differently. Innovative thinkers are those who push the boundaries of conventional wisdom, creating new paradigms and redefining success. This chapter explores some of the most remarkable minds who have exemplified innovative thinking in their fields, offering insights and inspiration for those aspiring to reach new heights in their professional endeavors.

1.   Steve Jobs: Revolutionizing Technology

Steve Jobs, the co-founder of Apple Inc., is a quintessential example of innovative thinking. His approach to technology was not merely about creating functional products but about designing experiences that seamlessly integrated into everyday life. Jobs' vision led to the development of revolutionary products such as the iPhone, iPad, and MacBook, which transformed the technology landscape.

Jobs' innovation lay not only in the products themselves but in his understanding of design and user experience. He famously focused on simplicity and elegance, creating devices that were intuitive and aesthetically pleasing. His ability to foresee the potential of technology in transforming how people interact with the world around them made him a pioneer of the digital age.

Key Takeaways:

Visionary thinking involves looking beyond current technologies and imagining their potential impact on the future.

Combining design with functionality can lead to groundbreaking innovations.

2.   Elon Musk: Pushing the Boundaries of Possibility

Elon Musk, the CEO of SpaceX and Tesla, is another prominent example of an innovative thinker. Musk's ventures span multiple industries, including aerospace, automotive, and renewable energy. His approach to innovation involves tackling some of the most significant challenges facing humanity, such as space exploration and sustainable energy.

Musk's work with SpaceX aims to make space travel more affordable and accessible, with the long-term goal of establishing a human presence on Mars. At Tesla, he has been at the forefront of developing electric vehicles and advancing battery technology, driving the shift towards sustainable transportation. Musk's ability to envision and pursue ambitious goals, often with a willingness to take substantial risks, underscores his role as a transformative force in modern technology.

Key Takeaways:
Addressing grand challenges can lead to revolutionary advancements.

Taking calculated risks and pursuing ambitious goals are essential for breakthrough innovations.

3.   Marie Curie: Breaking New Ground in Science
Marie Curie, the first woman to win a Nobel Prize and the only person to win Nobel Prizes in two different scientific fields, exemplifies groundbreaking innovation in science. Her pioneering work on radioactivity not only advanced scientific understanding but also led to practical applications in medicine and industry.

Curie's relentless pursuit of knowledge and her innovative research methods contributed to the development of X-ray machines, which revolutionized medical diagnostics. Her dedication to science in the face of numerous obstacles highlights the importance of perseverance and creativity in pushing the boundaries of what is known.

Key Takeaways:
Persistent research and dedication can lead to significant scientific advancements.

Innovations often emerge from challenging existing knowledge and exploring uncharted territories.

4. Jeff Bezos: Transforming Retail and Logistics

Jeff Bezos, the founder of Amazon, is a prime example of innovation in retail and logistics. His vision for Amazon was not just to create an online bookstore but to build a comprehensive e-commerce platform that could offer virtually any product. This vision evolved into Amazon's extensive range of services, including cloud computing, streaming, and logistics.

Bezos' focus on customer experience and operational efficiency led to innovations such as the development of Amazon Prime and the implementation of advanced logistics and delivery systems. His emphasis on data-driven decision-making and experimentation has been key to Amazon's continued growth and dominance in the global market.

Key Takeaways:
Innovating around customer needs can lead to significant business growth.
Leveraging technology and data can optimize operations and enhance service delivery.

5. Oprah Winfrey: Redefining Media and Personal Empowerment
Oprah Winfrey's career offers a compelling example of innovation in media and personal empowerment. From her beginnings as a television talk show host, Oprah transformed media by creating a platform that addressed personal and social issues, giving voice to a diverse range of perspectives.

Her innovative approach extended beyond traditional media formats with the launch of the Oprah Winfrey Network (OWN) and her book club, which significantly impacted publishing and media. Oprah's ability to connect with people on a personal level and use her platform for social change demonstrates how innovative thinking can redefine industries and inspire millions.

Key Takeaways:
Using media platforms to address broader social issues can create powerful change.

Connecting personally with audiences can amplify the impact of innovations.

6. Dr. Verghese Kurien: Revolutionizing Dairy Farming
Dr. Verghese Kurien, often referred to as the "Father of the White Revolution" in India, is a prime example of innovative thinking in agriculture and dairy farming. Kurien's vision was to transform India's dairy industry, which was primarily characterized by inefficiencies and low productivity.

Kurien's key innovation was the establishment of the Gujarat Cooperative Milk Marketing Federation (GCMMF), which later became famous for its Amul brand. By creating a cooperative model that empowered local dairy farmers, he introduced a system of milk collection, processing, and distribution that ensured fair prices for producers and high-quality products for consumers.

His approach included introducing new technology, improving milk production techniques, and establishing a robust supply chain. Kurien's model not only revolutionized dairy farming in India but also provided a framework for cooperative development in other sectors. His work has had a lasting impact on rural development and food security in India.

Key Takeaways:
Cooperative models can significantly enhance productivity and fairness in agricultural sectors.

Leveraging technology and efficient supply chains can transform traditional industries.

7. N. R. Narayana Murthy: Transforming the IT Industry
N. R. Narayana Murthy, co-founder of Infosys, is a notable example of innovative thinking in the information technology sector. Murthy's vision was to build a global IT services company from India that could compete with the best in the world. Under his leadership, Infosys

became a trailblazer in the IT industry, setting new standards for quality, ethics, and corporate governance.

Murthy's innovative strategies included adopting a unique business model focused on delivering high-quality software services and establishing strong ethical practices. Infosys was among the first Indian companies to adopt the "Global Delivery Model," which allowed them to provide services around the clock by leveraging teams in different time zones. This model became a benchmark for the IT industry.

Murthy also emphasized the importance of employee welfare and leadership development, fostering a culture of continuous learning and innovation. His contributions have played a crucial role in positioning India as a global IT hub and inspiring numerous startups and professionals.

Key Takeaways:
Innovative business models can set new industry standards and drive global competitiveness.

Emphasizing quality, ethics, and employee development is essential for sustained success.

Conclusion
These examples illustrate the diverse ways in which innovative thinking can drive professional excellence. These individuals have not only excelled in their fields but have also redefined the possibilities within their industries. By studying their approaches and applying similar principles of creativity, vision, and risk-taking, professionals can push beyond boundaries and achieve remarkable success in their own careers.

Chapter 18

LEADERSHIP AND TRAITS OF EFFECTIVE LEADERS

Introduction

Leadership is a dynamic force that propels organizations and individuals towards achieving their goals. Effective leadership is not merely about holding a position of authority but about inspiring and guiding others toward a common vision. This chapter delves into the essence of leadership, exploring the traits that define effective leaders and how these qualities can transcend boundaries to foster professional excellence.

Defining Leadership

At its core, leadership is the ability to influence and inspire others to achieve a shared objective. It encompasses vision, motivation, and the ability to navigate complex challenges. Effective leaders go beyond traditional notions of management; they shape the culture, drive innovation, and instill a sense of purpose within their teams.

Key Traits of Effective Leaders

Visionary Thinking

Effective leaders possess a clear vision of the future. They anticipate trends, set ambitious goals, and articulate a compelling vision that aligns with organizational objectives. This forward-thinking approach enables leaders to inspire their teams and drive sustained success.

Example: Steve Jobs' visionary approach transformed Apple into a tech giant. His ability to foresee the potential of personal computing and design a seamless user experience propelled Apple to unprecedented heights.

Empathy and Emotional Intelligence

Empathy is the cornerstone of effective leadership. Leaders who understand and relate to their team members' emotions and perspectives can foster trust, collaboration, and a positive work environment. Emotional intelligence enables leaders to manage their own emotions and navigate interpersonal relationships with sensitivity and insight.

Example: Satya Nadella's empathetic leadership at Microsoft was instrumental in reshaping the company's culture. His focus on empathy and inclusiveness led to a more collaborative and innovative work environment.

Decisiveness

The ability to make informed and timely decisions is crucial for effective leadership. Decisive leaders assess situations, weigh options, and take action confidently. They balance risk with opportunity, ensuring that their decisions drive progress and align with the overarching vision.

Example: Winston Churchill's decisive leadership during World War II was pivotal in rallying the British people and shaping the outcome of the conflict.

Integrity and Accountability

Integrity involves adhering to ethical principles and maintaining transparency in actions and decisions. Effective leaders are accountable for their actions and decisions, fostering a culture of trust and respect. They lead by example, demonstrating honesty and ethical behavior in all interactions.

Example: Nelson Mandela's unwavering integrity and commitment to justice earned him global respect and enabled him to lead South Africa through a period of profound change and reconciliation.

Adaptability and Resilience

In a rapidly changing world, adaptability is a crucial trait for leaders. Effective leaders embrace change, adjust strategies as needed, and remain resilient in the face of challenges. Their ability to pivot and maintain focus during adversity ensures that their teams stay aligned and motivated.

Example: Jeff Bezos' adaptability in shifting Amazon's focus from a bookstore to a global e-commerce and cloud computing leader showcases his ability to navigate and capitalize on changing market dynamics.

Communication Skills

Clear and effective communication is essential for leaders to convey their vision, provide feedback, and engage their teams. Strong communicators listen actively, articulate their messages clearly, and foster an open dialogue that encourages collaboration and innovation.

Example: Oprah Winfrey's exceptional communication skills have been instrumental in her success as a media mogul. Her ability to connect with people and convey authentic messages has inspired and influenced millions.

Delegation and Empowerment

Effective leaders understand the importance of delegation and empowering their team members. By delegating tasks and trusting their team's abilities, leaders foster growth, innovation, and a sense of ownership. Empowerment enhances team morale and leverages diverse skills and perspectives.

Example: Richard Branson's approach to delegation and empowerment at Virgin Group allowed his employees to take ownership of their roles, leading to a culture of innovation and entrepreneurial spirit.

Transcending Boundaries

Leadership excellence extends beyond organizational confines. Effective leaders transcend boundaries by influencing industry standards, shaping societal norms, and driving positive change. They leverage their traits to impact broader spheres, including social responsibility and global challenges.

Developing Leadership Traits

Developing leadership traits involves continuous self-assessment and growth. Leaders should seek feedback, engage in professional development, and cultivate self-awareness. Mentoring relationships and leadership training programs can also enhance these traits and contribute to personal and professional excellence.

Conclusion

Leadership is a multifaceted quality that encompasses vision, empathy, decisiveness, integrity, adaptability, communication, and empowerment. Effective leaders inspire and guide their teams, drive organizational success, and transcend boundaries to make a broader impact. By embodying these traits, leaders not only achieve professional excellence but also contribute to creating a more dynamic and inclusive world.

Chapter 19

LEADING BY EXAMPLE

Introduction

In the realm of professional excellence, leadership is often equated with the ability to inspire, guide, and influence others. However, one of the most potent and subtle forms of leadership is the act of leading by example. This principle transcends the mere act of managing tasks or directing teams; it involves embodying the values, work ethic, and standards you wish to see in others. This chapter delves into the significance of leading by example, how it fosters a culture of excellence, and practical strategies for implementing this powerful approach in your professional life.

The Essence of Leading by Example

Leading by example is not about perfect behavior or unattainable standards; it's about consistently demonstrating the values and principles you advocate. It's a commitment to practicing what you preach, thereby creating a blueprint for others to follow. This approach builds trust and credibility, as team members are more likely to respect and emulate leaders who live by the same rules they set.

Why Leading by Example Matters?

Establishes Credibility: When leaders adhere to the same standards they expect from their teams, they establish credibility. This authenticity fosters trust and respect, essential ingredients for effective leadership.

Encourages Accountability: Leading by example sets a benchmark for performance and behavior. It reinforces the idea that everyone is accountable for their actions and that standards apply uniformly across all levels of the organization.

Fosters a Positive Culture: Leaders who model positive behaviors—such as integrity, diligence, and empathy—help cultivate a supportive and productive work environment. This positive culture enhances morale and motivates others to strive for excellence.

Drives Change: Leading by example is a powerful tool for driving change. Leaders who adopt new practices or embrace innovation demonstrate the benefits and feasibility of these changes, encouraging others to follow suit.

Practical Strategies for Leading by Example

Align Actions with Values: Ensure that your actions consistently reflect the values and principles you advocate. If you promote transparency, for instance, be open and honest in your communications and decision-making processes.

Demonstrate Work Ethic: Exhibit a strong work ethic by being punctual, diligent, and committed. Your dedication to excellence will inspire others to emulate these qualities in their own work.

Practice Empathy and Respect: Show genuine concern for your team members' well-being and respect their contributions. Your empathetic approach will foster a supportive atmosphere where individuals feel valued and motivated.

Embrace Continuous Learning: Commit to personal and professional growth by seeking feedback, pursuing further education, and adapting to new challenges. Your willingness to learn and improve sets a powerful example for others to follow.

Handle Challenges Gracefully: Demonstrate resilience and composure in the face of adversity. Your ability to navigate difficulties with grace and a solutions-oriented mindset will inspire your team to approach challenges with a similar attitude.

Challenges and Considerations

Leading by example is not without its challenges. Leaders must be vigilant about maintaining consistency, as lapses in behavior can undermine their credibility. Additionally, it requires a high level of self-awareness and emotional intelligence to effectively model the desired behaviors.

Conclusion

Leading by example is a cornerstone of professional excellence. It involves embodying the values and behaviors you wish to see in others, thereby creating a culture of trust, accountability, and excellence. By aligning your actions with your principles, demonstrating a strong work ethic, and fostering a positive environment, you inspire those around you to reach their full potential. As you navigate your professional journey, remember that the most effective leaders are those who lead not just with their words, but with their actions.

Chapter 20

STORIES OF LEADERS WHO BROKE BARRIERS

Introduction

In the journey of professional excellence, many individuals have faced daunting barriers—societal norms, corporate ceilings, and personal limitations. Yet, some have not only confronted these challenges but have transcended them, setting new paradigms of success and inspiring countless others. This chapter explores the stories of leaders who have broken barriers, illustrating the power of resilience, innovation, and unwavering determination.

1. Ursula Burns: Breaking the Glass Ceiling

Ursula Burns made history as the first African American woman to lead a Fortune 500 company, Xerox. Born and raised in a New York City housing project, Burns faced numerous challenges growing up. However, her mother instilled in her a strong work ethic and the importance of education. Burns joined Xerox as an intern and worked her way up through various engineering and management roles. Her ascension to CEO was not just a personal achievement but a monumental step for diversity and inclusion in corporate America. Burns championed innovation and steered Xerox through a significant transformation, proving that leadership is not confined by gender or race.

2. Elon Musk: Redefining Industries

Elon Musk, the founder of SpaceX and Tesla, is a quintessential example of a leader who breaks barriers. Musk's vision of space exploration and sustainable energy has challenged and reshaped entire industries. Despite numerous setbacks, including early failures of SpaceX rockets and financial struggles at Tesla, Musk's relentless pursuit of his goals has led to groundbreaking advancements. SpaceX's development of reusable rockets and Tesla's leadership in electric vehicles demonstrate how visionary thinking can overcome technical and financial obstacles, ultimately transforming the world.

3. Indra Nooyi: Leadership with Empathy

Indra Nooyi, former CEO of PepsiCo, is celebrated not only for her business acumen but also for her empathetic leadership style. Nooyi, who was born in India and moved to the United States for higher education, navigated the complex dynamics of global business with grace. During her tenure at PepsiCo, she prioritized sustainable growth and health-conscious products, balancing profitability with social responsibility. Nooyi's emphasis on diversity and inclusion within the company set new standards for corporate leadership, showcasing how breaking barriers often involves creating new, more inclusive paradigms.

4. Satya Nadella: Transforming Microsoft

Satya Nadella's journey to becoming the CEO of Microsoft is a testament to the power of adaptive leadership. Taking the helm in 2014, Nadella faced the challenge of revitalizing a tech giant that was seen as lagging behind its competitors. He shifted Microsoft's focus to cloud computing and embraced a culture of continuous learning and innovation. Nadella's leadership broke the barrier of a stagnant corporate culture, fostering an environment where empathy and collaboration drive technological advancement. His story underscores the importance of agility and vision in overcoming organizational inertia.

5. Malala Yousafzai: Advocacy Through Education

Though not a business leader in the traditional sense, Malala Yousafzai's impact on education and women's rights is a powerful example of breaking barriers. After surviving a Taliban assassination attempt for advocating girls' education in Pakistan, Malala has become a global symbol of resilience and courage. Her story illustrates how leadership is not confined to boardrooms and offices but can also thrive in the face of extreme adversity. Malala's advocacy has mobilized millions worldwide, breaking the barriers of ignorance and oppression through education and empowerment.

6. Jack Ma: From Rejection to Global Influence

Jack Ma, the co-founder of Alibaba Group, faced numerous rejections early in his career, including being turned down for jobs at KFC and the police force. Despite these setbacks, Ma remained undeterred and pursued his vision of creating a global e-commerce platform. Alibaba's success has redefined the landscape of online commerce, particularly in

China. Ma's story is a reminder that perseverance in the face of repeated failure can lead to monumental success. His leadership broke barriers not just in business but also in technology and international trade.

7. Sundar Pichai: Leading Google to New Heights

Sundar Pichai, the CEO of Alphabet Inc. and its subsidiary Google, is another remarkable leader who has broken barriers. Born in Chennai, India, Pichai's journey from a modest background to the helm of one of the world's most influential companies is truly inspiring. After joining Google in 2004, Pichai played pivotal roles in developing key products like Chrome, Chrome OS, and Google Drive. His ability to lead complex projects and his innovative thinking led to his appointment as CEO in 2015. Pichai's leadership has been marked by a focus on artificial intelligence and expanding Google's product offerings, showcasing how embracing technology and innovation can drive global success.

8. Kiran Mazumdar-Shaw: Pioneering Biotechnology in India

Kiran Mazumdar-Shaw, the founder and chairperson of Biocon Limited, is a trailblazer in the field of biotechnology. Facing gender biases and skepticism in a male-dominated industry, Mazumdar-Shaw started Biocon in 1978 with limited resources and turned it into one of India's leading biotechnology companies. Her relentless pursuit of innovation and excellence has led to significant advancements in affordable healthcare and the development of biosimilars. Mazumdar-Shaw's story is a testament to the impact of resilience, vision, and commitment to societal betterment, breaking barriers in both business and science.

Conclusion

The stories of these leaders—Ursula Burns, Elon Musk, Indra Nooyi, Satya Nadella, Malala Yousafzai, Jack Ma, Sundar Pichai, and Kiran Mazumdar-Shaw—illustrate that breaking barriers is a multifaceted endeavor. It requires vision, resilience, empathy, and a willingness to challenge the status quo. These individuals have not only achieved professional excellence but have also paved the way for others to follow, inspiring a new generation of leaders to go beyond boundaries in their own journeys. Through their examples, we learn that the greatest achievements often arise from the most significant challenges, and that true leadership is about making a lasting impact that transcends personal and professional barriers.

Chapter 21

WORK-LIFE BALANCE

Introduction

In the relentless pursuit of professional excellence, the concept of work-life balance often becomes an elusive ideal. Many professionals find themselves entangled in the demanding web of their careers, leaving little room for personal well-being, family, and leisure. Achieving a harmonious balance between work and personal life is crucial for long-term success and fulfillment. This chapter explores the significance of work-life balance, practical strategies to attain it, and inspiring stories of individuals who have mastered this equilibrium.

The Importance of Work-Life Balance

Work-life balance is more than just a trendy buzzword; it is a vital component of a healthy, productive, and fulfilling life. The benefits of maintaining a balance between professional and personal spheres include:

1. **Enhanced Productivity:** A well-balanced life fosters greater focus, creativity, and efficiency at work. When employees are not overwhelmed by stress or burnout, they perform better and contribute more effectively to their organizations.

2. **Improved Health and Well-being:** Chronic stress from an imbalanced lifestyle can lead to various health issues, including anxiety, depression, and cardiovascular diseases. Prioritizing personal time and self-care promotes better physical and mental health.

3. **Stronger Relationships:** Devoting time to family and friends strengthens personal bonds and provides emotional support. These relationships are crucial for personal happiness and resilience.

4. **Increased Job Satisfaction:** Employees who achieve work-life balance tend to be more satisfied with their jobs. They feel valued by their employers, which leads to higher morale and loyalty.

Strategies for Achieving Work-Life Balance

Achieving work-life balance requires intentional effort and mindful practices. Here are some practical strategies to help you navigate the delicate balance between work and personal life:

1. **Set Clear Boundaries:** Establishing boundaries between work and personal life is essential. Define specific work hours and stick to them. Avoid checking work emails or taking business calls during personal time.

2. **Prioritize Tasks:** Use effective time management techniques to prioritize tasks. Focus on high-impact activities and delegate or eliminate non-essential tasks. This approach helps in managing workloads without feeling overwhelmed.

3. **Learn to Say No:** It is important to recognize your limits and avoid overcommitting. Politely declining additional work or social obligations allows you to maintain a manageable schedule.

4. **Embrace Flexibility:** Flexible work arrangements, such as remote work or flexible hours, can significantly improve work-life balance. Explore options with your employer that accommodate both your professional and personal needs.

5. **Practice Self-Care:** Prioritize self-care activities, such as exercise, meditation, hobbies, and adequate sleep. Taking care of your physical and mental well-being enhances your ability to handle work pressures.

6. **Seek Support:** Don't hesitate to seek support from family, friends, or colleagues. Sharing responsibilities and seeking advice can alleviate stress and provide different perspectives on managing work-life balance.

7. **Unplug Regularly:** Designate times to unplug from technology and disconnect from work-related communications. This digital detox allows you to be fully present in your personal life.

Inspiring Stories of Work-Life Balance
Case Study 1: Sheryl Sandberg
Sheryl Sandberg, COO of Facebook and author of "Lean In," is an inspiring example of someone who has achieved work-life balance. Despite her demanding role in a leading tech company, Sandberg prioritizes family time and openly discusses the importance of leaving work at a reasonable hour to be with her children. Her transparency and advocacy for work-life balance have influenced corporate cultures worldwide.

Case Study 2: Arianna Huffington
Arianna Huffington, co-founder of The Huffington Post and founder of Thrive Global, experienced burnout firsthand, leading her to champion the importance of well-being and work-life balance. Through her work at Thrive Global, she promotes strategies for reducing stress and enhancing personal fulfillment, proving that success and balance are not mutually exclusive.

Conclusion
Achieving work-life balance is a continuous journey that requires dedication, mindfulness, and flexibility. By setting clear boundaries, prioritizing tasks, and embracing self-care, individuals can attain a harmonious balance that enhances both professional performance and personal satisfaction. The inspiring stories of leaders like Sheryl Sandberg, Satya Nadella, and Arianna Huffington demonstrate that it is possible to excel in your career while nurturing a fulfilling personal life.
Work-life balance is not a destination but a dynamic process. As you navigate the complexities of professional excellence, remember to prioritize your well-being and cherish the moments that matter most

Chapter 22

THE IMPORTANCE OF BALANCE FOR SUCCESS

Introduction

In the quest for success, balance often appears as a secondary concern. However, the most accomplished individuals understand that true success is not just about excelling in one area of life but maintaining harmony across multiple domains. This chapter delves into the critical role balance plays in achieving sustainable success, exploring its impact on personal well-being, professional performance, and overall life satisfaction.

The Multifaceted Nature of Success

Success is a multifaceted concept that extends beyond professional achievements. It encompasses personal growth, relationships, health, and happiness. Balancing these aspects is essential for holistic success:

1. **Personal Well-being:** Physical and mental health are foundational to success. Without maintaining balance in these areas, it becomes challenging to sustain high performance and long-term achievements.

2. **Professional Excellence:** Career success is undoubtedly important, but it should not come at the expense of other life areas. Balanced professionals are more creative, efficient, and resilient, leading to greater career satisfaction and achievement.

3. **Relationships:** Strong relationships with family, friends, and colleagues provide emotional support and enrich life experiences. A balanced approach to nurturing these connections fosters a supportive network that is crucial during challenging times.

4. **Hobbies and Interests:** Engaging in activities outside of work promotes creativity, reduces stress, and enhances overall life satisfaction. Hobbies and interests provide a necessary counterbalance to professional responsibilities.

The Benefits of Balance

Maintaining balance in life offers numerous benefits that contribute to sustainable success:

1. **Enhanced Creativity and Problem-Solving:** A balanced life allows for diverse experiences and perspectives, which fuel creativity and innovative thinking. Time away from work often leads to fresh insights and solutions to professional challenges.

2. **Improved Health and Well-being:** Balance promotes better physical and mental health, reducing the risk of burnout, anxiety, and other stress-related issues. Healthy individuals are more productive, focused, and capable of handling life's demands.

3. **Greater Resilience:** A balanced approach to life builds resilience. When one area of life faces challenges, other balanced aspects provide stability and support, enabling individuals to navigate difficulties more effectively.

4. **Sustained Motivation:** Balance prevents burnout and keeps motivation levels high. By allocating time to various life aspects, individuals maintain enthusiasm and energy for their professional pursuits.

Strategies for Achieving Balance

Achieving balance requires intentional effort and mindful practices. Here are some strategies to help you cultivate balance in your life:

1. **Set Priorities:** Identify what matters most in your life and allocate time accordingly. Ensure that your schedule reflects your values and priorities, balancing work, family, health, and personal interests.

2. **Establish Boundaries:** Clearly define the boundaries between work and personal life. Avoid letting professional demands encroach on personal time, and vice versa.

3. **Practice Time Management:** Use effective time management techniques to organize your tasks and responsibilities. Prioritize important activities and avoid overcommitting.

4. **Delegate and Collaborate:** don't hesitate to delegate tasks at work and home. Collaboration and delegation reduce stress and free up time for other important areas of life.

5. **Schedule Downtime:** Intentionally schedule time for relaxation and leisure. Downtime is essential for recharging and maintaining overall well-being.

6. **Stay Mindful:** Mindfulness practices, such as meditation and deep breathing, help maintain balance by keeping you present and focused. Regular mindfulness exercises enhance emotional regulation and stress management.

Inspiring Examples of Balanced Success

Case Study 1: Richard Branson

Richard Branson, founder of the Virgin Group, is known for his adventurous spirit and business acumen. Despite leading a vast business empire, Branson prioritizes personal well-being and family time. He believes that maintaining balance is key to his creativity and success, often engaging in adventurous activities that provide a counterbalance to his professional responsibilities.

Case Study 2: Bill Gates

Bill Gates, co-founder of Microsoft, has demonstrated a balanced approach to success. After stepping down from his day-to-day role at Microsoft, Gates dedicated his time to philanthropic efforts through the Bill & Melinda Gates Foundation. His ability to balance business success with impactful philanthropy showcases the importance of maintaining harmony in various life aspects.

Conclusion

Balance is a cornerstone of sustainable success. It is not merely about dividing time equally among different areas of life but about creating harmony that enhances overall well-being and performance. By setting priorities, establishing boundaries, practicing time management, and staying mindful, individuals can achieve a balanced life that fosters personal growth, professional excellence, and lasting fulfillment.

Chapter 23

CASE STUDIES OF SUCCESSFUL WORK-LIFE INTEGRATION

Introduction

Work-life integration is more than a strategy; it is a philosophy that embraces the fluidity between professional responsibilities and personal aspirations. Unlike the traditional concept of work-life balance, which often implies a strict separation between work and life, work-life integration acknowledges that the two can coexist harmoniously. This chapter presents compelling case studies of individuals who have successfully integrated their work and personal lives, demonstrating that professional excellence and personal fulfillment can be achieved simultaneously.

Case Study 1: Shonda Rhimes

Background: Shonda Rhimes is a prolific television producer, screenwriter, and author, best known for creating hit shows like Grey's Anatomy and Scandal. As a single mother of three, Rhimes faced the daunting task of managing a demanding career and her family life.

Work-Life Integration Strategies:

1. **Prioritizing Joy:** In her book Year of Yes, Rhimes shares her journey of saying yes to opportunities that bring joy and fulfillment. This mindset shift allowed her to integrate personal happiness with her professional responsibilities.

2. **Delegation:** Rhimes built a strong team that she trusts, enabling her to delegate tasks and responsibilities effectively. This practice allowed her to focus on strategic decisions and creative work while ensuring that her shows continued to run smoothly.

3. **Creating Family Time:** Despite her hectic schedule, Rhimes makes it a point to be present for her children. She blocks out specific times

for family activities, ensuring that her professional commitments do not overshadow her role as a mother.

Outcome: Rhimes's approach to work-life integration has enabled her to maintain a successful career while enjoying a fulfilling personal life. Her ability to prioritize joy and delegate effectively serves as an inspiration for many working parents.

Case Study 2: Jeff Weiner

Background: Jeff Weiner, the former CEO of LinkedIn, is known for his compassionate leadership style and emphasis on work-life integration. Weiner's approach to leadership and personal well-being has been instrumental in shaping LinkedIn's culture.

Work-Life Integration Strategies:

1. **Mindful Leadership:** Weiner practices and advocates for mindfulness, encouraging his team to incorporate mindfulness into their daily routines. This practice enhances focus, reduces stress, and fosters a supportive work environment.

2. **Open Communication:** Weiner promotes open communication about work-life integration within the organization. By fostering a culture where employees feel comfortable discussing their needs and challenges, LinkedIn has created a more inclusive and supportive workplace.

3. **Personal Well-being:** Weiner prioritizes his well-being by maintaining a regular exercise routine, spending time with family, and engaging in activities that recharge him. This personal commitment to well-being sets a positive example for his team.

Outcome: Under Weiner's leadership, LinkedIn has thrived, becoming one of the most sought-after workplaces. His commitment to mindfulness and open communication has not only benefited his personal life but also fostered a positive and productive organizational culture.

Case Study 3: Marissa Mayer

Background: Marissa Mayer, former CEO of Yahoo and a key player at Google, is known for her intense work ethic and dedication to her career. Despite the demanding nature of her roles, Mayer has managed to integrate her professional and personal lives.

Work-Life Integration Strategies:

1. **Blurring Boundaries:** Mayer integrates her work and personal life by allowing them to overlap. She often brings her children to the office and incorporates family activities into her workday, demonstrating that work and family can coexist.

2. **Time Management:** Mayer is known for her meticulous time management skills. She allocates specific time blocks for different activities, ensuring that she can fulfill both her professional and personal responsibilities effectively.

3. **Support Systems:** Mayer relies on a strong support system, including family, friends, and professional help, to manage her responsibilities. This network provides the necessary assistance and support, enabling her to focus on her career and family.

Outcome: Mayer's approach to work-life integration has allowed her to achieve significant professional success while maintaining her personal commitments. Her ability to blur the boundaries between work and life serves as a model for individuals striving for integration in their lives.

Case Study 4: Satya Nadella

Background: Satya Nadella, CEO of Microsoft, is renowned for his empathetic leadership and commitment to work-life integration. Nadella's personal experiences, including raising a special-needs child, have profoundly influenced his approach to work and life.

Work-Life Integration Strategies:

1. **Empathy and Inclusion:** Nadella emphasizes empathy and inclusion in Microsoft's culture, recognizing the diverse needs of employees. This approach has led to policies that support work-life integration, such as flexible work hours and remote work options.

2. **Leading by Example:** Nadella openly shares his experiences and challenges related to work-life integration, encouraging employees to prioritize their well-being. His transparency fosters a culture of trust and understanding within the organization.

3. **Family Time:** Despite his demanding role, Nadella prioritizes family time and personal well-being. He ensures that his professional commitments do not overshadow his responsibilities as a husband and father.

Outcome: Nadella's leadership has transformed Microsoft, fostering a culture of empathy, inclusion, and work-life integration. His approach has not only enhanced employee satisfaction and productivity but also solidified Microsoft's reputation as a forward-thinking and compassionate company.

Case Study 5: Indra Nooyi

Background: Indra Nooyi, former CEO of PepsiCo, is celebrated for her transformative leadership and dedication to work-life integration. As a mother and a top executive, Nooyi has often discussed the challenges and strategies involved in balancing her roles.

Work-Life Integration Strategies:

1. **Transparent Communication:** Nooyi has been open about the struggles and realities of managing a demanding career while raising a family. Her honesty has encouraged a more realistic dialogue about work-life integration in corporate environments.

2. **Support Networks:** Nooyi credits a strong support network, including her family and professional mentors, for helping her navigate the complexities of her dual roles. This network has been crucial in providing emotional and logistical support.

3. **Workplace Policies:** Under Nooyi's leadership, PepsiCo implemented policies that support work-life integration, such as flexible working hours and parental leave, promoting a culture where employees can achieve both professional and personal goals.

Outcome: Nooyi's balanced approach has led to her remarkable success at PepsiCo while maintaining a fulfilling personal life. Her leadership has inspired many organizations to adopt more supportive work-life policies.

Case Study 6: Ratan Tata

Background: Ratan Tata, former chairman of Tata Sons, is a revered figure in Indian business, known for his humility, philanthropic efforts, and balanced approach to life. Tata has managed to integrate his extensive professional responsibilities with his personal interests and commitments.

Work-Life Integration Strategies:

1. **Philanthropy and Personal Passion:** Tata has seamlessly integrated his professional role with his philanthropic passions. Through the Tata Trusts, he has been able to contribute significantly to social causes, aligning his professional success with personal fulfillment.

2. **Maintaining Humility:** Despite his success, Tata has always emphasized the importance of humility and personal integrity. This attitude has helped him maintain a grounded perspective, balancing his personal values with his professional ambitions.

3. **Personal Interests:** Tata's interest in automobiles and aviation has provided a creative outlet beyond his corporate responsibilities. Engaging in these personal hobbies has helped him maintain a balanced and enriched life.

Outcome: Ratan Tata's ability to integrate his professional achievements with personal passions and philanthropic efforts has set a powerful example of holistic success. His balanced approach has earned him immense respect and admiration worldwide.

Conclusion

The stories of Shonda Rhimes, Jeff Weiner, Marissa Mayer, Satya Nadella, Indra Nooyi, and Ratan Tata illustrate that successful work-life integration is achievable with intentional strategies and a supportive environment. These leaders have demonstrated that it is possible to excel professionally while maintaining personal fulfillment and well-being.

Work-life integration is not about finding a perfect balance but about creating a harmonious blend of work and personal life that suits individual needs and circumstances. As you navigate your professional journey, draw inspiration from these case studies and embrace the philosophy of work-life integration to achieve a fulfilling and successful life beyond boundaries.

PART III
Social Impact beyond Boundaries

Chapter 24

COMMUNITY BUILDING

Introduction

In a world increasingly interconnected yet often marked by fragmentation, the concept of community building emerges as a vital force. It transcends mere geographical proximity, encompassing shared values, mutual support, and collective growth. This chapter delves into the essence of community building, exploring its profound impact on social dynamics, individual well-being, and broader societal progress.

1. The Essence of Community

A community is more than a group of individuals; it is a living, evolving entity shaped by common goals, shared experiences, and mutual respect. The sense of belonging within a community fosters emotional security, enabling individuals to thrive. In this interconnected web, the strength of relationships and the quality of interactions determine the community's resilience and vibrancy.

2. Historical Perspectives on Community Building

Throughout history, communities have been the bedrock of human civilization. From ancient tribes to modern urban societies, the principles of cooperation, shared resources, and collective problem-solving have driven progress. Historical examples, such as the agricultural communities of Mesopotamia or the guilds of medieval Europe, illustrate how collaborative efforts have laid the foundations for societal advancement.

3. The Role of Leadership in Community Building

Effective community building requires visionary leadership. Leaders who inspire, unite, and empower individuals can transform disparate groups into cohesive communities. Such leaders often exhibit empathy, inclusivity, and a genuine commitment to the collective good. Through their actions and words, they cultivate trust, foster open communication, and encourage active participation.

4. Strategies for Effective Community Building

To build a thriving community, several key strategies must be employed:

Inclusivity: Embrace diversity and ensure that every member feels valued and heard. An inclusive community harnesses the strengths of its varied members, leading to richer, more innovative solutions.

Shared Vision: Develop a clear, collective vision that aligns with the community's values and goals. This vision serves as a guiding star, motivating and uniting members in their endeavors.

Active Participation: Encourage active engagement from all members. Participation fosters a sense of ownership and accountability, driving collective efforts toward common objectives.

Open Communication: Establish channels for transparent and respectful communication. Open dialogue allows for the exchange of ideas, resolution of conflicts, and reinforcement of trust.

Support Systems: Create mechanisms for mutual support, whether through formal structures like support groups or informal networks of assistance. A supportive community enhances individual well-being and collective resilience.

5. The Impact of Technology on Community Building

In the digital age, technology has revolutionized the way communities are formed and maintained. Online platforms enable the creation of virtual communities that transcend geographical boundaries. Social media, forums, and collaborative tools facilitate connection, information sharing, and collective action. However, the digital realm also presents challenges, such as the potential for superficial interactions and the risk of exclusion for those without access to technology. Balancing digital and face-to-face interactions is crucial for holistic community building.

6. Case Studies of Successful Community Building

The Grameen Bank: Founded by Nobel laureate Muhammad Yunus, the Grameen Bank in Bangladesh exemplifies successful community building through microfinance. By providing small loans to the impoverished, the bank empowered individuals, particularly women, fostering economic independence and community development.

Habitat for Humanity: This global nonprofit organization builds homes for those in need, relying on the collective effort of volunteers and future homeowners. The process not only provides shelter but also strengthens community bonds and instills a sense of pride and ownership.

Community-Supported Agriculture (CSA): CSA initiatives connect farmers with consumers who invest in their produce. This model supports local agriculture, promotes sustainable practices, and builds strong relationships between producers and consumers, fostering a sense of shared responsibility and mutual benefit.

7. The Role of Education in Community Building

Education plays a pivotal role in nurturing the skills, values, and attitudes essential for community building. Schools and educational institutions can act as microcosms of the larger community, promoting inclusivity, empathy, and civic engagement. Curriculum and extracurricular activities that emphasize collaboration, social responsibility, and critical thinking prepare individuals to contribute effectively to their communities.

8. Overcoming Challenges in Community Building

Building and sustaining a community is not without challenges. Conflicts, differing interests, and external pressures can strain the fabric of a community. Effective conflict resolution strategies, adaptability, and a focus on common goals are essential for overcoming these obstacles. Continuous reflection and dialogue help communities evolve and strengthen over time.

9. The Future of Community Building

As societies become increasingly complex, the need for robust, adaptable communities grows. Future community building efforts must prioritize sustainability, inclusivity, and innovation. Embracing new technologies, fostering cross-cultural understanding, and promoting global citizenship will be critical in shaping resilient communities capable of addressing the challenges of the 21st century.

Conclusion

Community building is a dynamic, ongoing process that enriches individuals and society as a whole. By fostering connections, nurturing mutual support, and striving for collective well-being, we can create communities that transcend boundaries and drive positive social impact. As we navigate the complexities of the modern world, the principles of community building offer a powerful framework for creating a more inclusive, resilient, and harmonious society.

Chapter 25

THE POWER OF COLLECTIVE EFFORT

Introduction

In our journey beyond personal and professional growth, we inevitably encounter the profound influence of collective effort. Human history is replete with examples of communities, societies, and movements that have achieved remarkable feats through unified action. From the civil rights movements to modern technological advancements, the power of collective effort has driven social impact, transforming the fabric of our world. In this chapter, we explore the essence of collective effort, how it shapes our social environment, and the strategies to harness this power for greater good.

The Essence of Collective Effort

Collective effort is the collaborative energy that arises when individuals come together, driven by a shared vision or common goal. This synergy creates a force far greater than the sum of its parts, enabling the group to overcome challenges, innovate, and effect change on a grand scale. The essence of collective effort lies in:

Shared Vision: A clear, compelling vision that resonates with the group, providing direction and purpose.

Collaborative Spirit: An environment where each member's strengths and perspectives are valued and utilized.

Mutual Support: A network of encouragement and assistance, fostering resilience and perseverance.

Shared Responsibility: A sense of ownership and accountability towards the collective goal.

Historical Examples of Collective Effort

Throughout history, collective effort has been the bedrock of social progress and transformation. Consider the following examples:

1. **The Civil Rights Movement**

In the 1950s and 60s, the Civil Rights Movement in the United States epitomized the power of collective effort. Led by figures like Martin Luther King Jr., thousands of individuals unified in their pursuit of equality and justice. Through peaceful protests, legal challenges, and widespread advocacy, the movement dismantled institutionalized racial segregation and discrimination, leading to significant legislative and societal changes.

2. **The Indian Independence Movement**

The Indian independence movement, spearheaded by Mahatma Gandhi and other leaders, mobilized millions in a non-violent struggle against British colonial rule. The collective effort of diverse groups and communities, united in their quest for self-rule, ultimately culminated in India's independence in 1947.

3. **The Global Environmental Movement**

In recent decades, the environmental movement has highlighted the urgent need for collective action to address climate change and environmental degradation. Organizations like Greenpeace, the World Wildlife Fund, and countless grassroots movements worldwide have galvanized public awareness and policy changes, emphasizing that the health of our planet hinges on unified, global efforts.

The Dynamics of Effective Collective Effort

To harness the power of collective effort, certain dynamics must be nurtured within a group:

1. **Inclusive Leadership**

Effective collective efforts often benefit from inclusive leadership, where leaders facilitate collaboration, empower individuals, and foster an environment of mutual respect and inclusivity. Inclusive leaders prioritize the group's vision over personal agendas and encourage participatory decision-making.

2. **Open Communication**

Transparent and open communication is crucial in maintaining trust and unity within a group. Regular dialogue ensures that all members are informed, heard, and engaged. It helps in resolving conflicts, aligning efforts, and adapting to evolving circumstances.

3. Diverse Skill Sets
A diverse team brings a wealth of perspectives, skills, and ideas to the table. Encouraging diversity within a group not only enhances creativity and problem-solving but also ensures a more comprehensive approach to achieving the collective goal.

4. Shared Resources
Pooling resources, whether they are financial, informational, or human, amplifies the impact of collective efforts. Shared resources enable the group to leverage each member's contributions effectively, avoiding redundancy and maximizing efficiency.

5. Continuous Learning
Groups that prioritize continuous learning and adaptation remain resilient in the face of challenges. Embracing feedback, reflecting on experiences, and staying open to new ideas help the group evolve and stay aligned with its vision.

Strategies to Foster Collective Effort
To leverage collective effort for social impact, consider implementing the following strategies:

1. Cultivate a Shared Vision
Begin by establishing a clear, inspiring vision that aligns with the values and aspirations of the group. Ensure that this vision is communicated effectively and consistently, creating a sense of purpose and direction.

2. Build Strong Relationships
Invest in building strong, trust-based relationships within the group. Foster a culture of empathy, respect, and support, where members feel valued and connected to the collective mission.

3. Encourage Active Participation
Create opportunities for all members to actively contribute to the group's efforts. Encourage participation in decision-making processes,

task assignments, and brainstorming sessions, ensuring that diverse voices are heard and considered.

4. Recognize and Celebrate Achievements

Acknowledge and celebrate the group's achievements, both big and small. Recognizing individual and collective contributions boosts morale, reinforces commitment, and fosters a sense of pride and ownership.

5. Facilitate Collaboration

Implement structures and practices that facilitate collaboration, such as regular meetings, collaborative tools, and shared spaces. Encourage cross-functional teamwork and the exchange of ideas to enhance synergy and innovation.

Case Study: The Power of Collective Effort in Action

The Success of the "Black Lives Matter" Movement

The "Black Lives Matter" (BLM) movement, which began in 2013, is a contemporary example of collective effort driving social change. Sparked by the acquittal of Trayvon Martin's killer, BLM has grown into a global movement advocating against systemic racism and violence towards Black people.

The movement's success can be attributed to its decentralized structure, inclusive leadership, and effective use of social media. BLM has galvanized millions worldwide, leading to policy changes, increased awareness, and a shift in public discourse on racial justice.

Conclusion

The power of collective effort is a testament to the profound impact that unified, collaborative action can have on society. By embracing shared vision, inclusive leadership, and open communication, we can harness this power to drive social change and make a lasting difference. As we move forward in our journey beyond boundaries, let us remember that together, we are capable of achieving extraordinary feats, transforming our world for the better.

Chapter 26

INITIATIVES THAT MADE A DIFFERENCE

Introduction

In a world where social challenges abound, the difference between stagnation and progress often hinges on the initiatives taken by dedicated individuals and organizations. These initiatives, regardless of their scale, can transform communities, improve lives, and inspire others to join the cause. This chapter delves into various initiatives that have made a substantial impact, showcasing the power of collective effort and the potential for positive change.

1. Education for All: Bridging the Gap

One of the most profound initiatives in recent years has been the global push for inclusive education. Organizations like Room to Read and Teach for All have dedicated themselves to ensuring that children, especially girls, in underprivileged regions receive quality education. These initiatives have built schools, trained teachers, and provided learning materials, significantly increasing literacy rates and empowering young minds to dream beyond their circumstances.

Case Study: Malala Fund

The Malala Fund, founded by Nobel laureate Malala Yousafzai, exemplifies the transformative power of education. By advocating for girls' education in regions plagued by conflict and gender discrimination, the Fund has helped millions of girls access education. Malala's story of resilience and her relentless advocacy have inspired global movements, demonstrating how one voice can spark monumental change.

2. Healthcare Accessibility: Healing Hands

Healthcare is a fundamental right, yet millions lack access to basic medical services. Initiatives like Doctors Without Borders and the Gates Foundation's healthcare projects have brought medical care to the most remote and underserved areas. These initiatives have tackled epidemics, provided vaccinations, and built healthcare infrastructure, saving countless lives and improving public health.

Case Study: VHCA Hair Clinic's Healthy Hair Movement

VHCA Hair Clinic, under the leadership of Dr. Mukesh Aggarwal, launched the Healthy Hair Movement to promote awareness and treatment of hair health issues through Ayurveda. By offering free consultations, affordable treatments, and educational programs, this initiative has helped thousands regain their confidence and health, highlighting the impact of accessible and holistic healthcare.

3. Environmental Conservation: Protecting Our Planet

The urgency of environmental conservation has led to numerous impactful initiatives aimed at preserving our planet. Organizations like the World Wildlife Fund (WWF) and Greenpeace have been at the forefront of efforts to combat deforestation, protect endangered species, and promote sustainable practices. These initiatives are crucial in the fight against climate change and biodiversity loss.

Case Study: The Great Green Wall

The Great Green Wall initiative in Africa aims to combat desertification by creating a mosaic of green and productive landscapes across the Sahel region. This ambitious project not only addresses environmental degradation but also fosters economic development and food security for millions. By restoring 100 million hectares of degraded land, the initiative is a testament to the power of large-scale environmental efforts.

4. Social Justice and Equality: Voices for the Voiceless

Social justice initiatives strive to rectify systemic inequalities and uplift marginalized communities. Movements such as Black Lives Matter and campaigns by Amnesty International have brought global attention to issues of racial injustice, human rights abuses, and gender inequality. These initiatives leverage advocacy, policy change, and community support to create a more equitable society.

Case Study: Me Too Movement

The #MeToo movement, founded by Tarana Burke and popularized globally, has shed light on the pervasive issue of sexual harassment and assault. By providing a platform for survivors to share their stories, the movement has ignited a global conversation and led to significant changes in workplace policies, legal frameworks, and societal attitudes towards gender-based violence.

5. Rural Development: Transforming Villages

Rural development initiatives in India have aimed to uplift and transform the socio-economic landscape of villages. These initiatives address various aspects such as agriculture, sanitation, education, and infrastructure, thereby improving the overall quality of life for rural populations. Organizations like the Barefoot College and the Art of Living's rural development programs have been instrumental in this transformation.

Case Study: Barefoot College

Founded by Bunker Roy, Barefoot College empowers rural communities by training villagers in sustainable professions. One of its notable programs trains women, often referred to as "Solar Mamas," to become solar engineers. These women install and maintain solar lighting systems in their villages, providing a sustainable energy source and reducing dependency on kerosene lamps. This initiative not only brings light to remote areas but also empowers women with technical skills and economic opportunities.

6. Digital Inclusion: Bridging the Digital Divide

In an era where digital connectivity is crucial, initiatives to bridge the digital divide in India have been transformative. The Digital India campaign, launched by the Government of India, aims to ensure that digital technology benefits all citizens, especially those in rural and underserved areas. This initiative focuses on improving digital infrastructure, increasing internet connectivity, and promoting digital literacy.

Case Study: e-Choupal by ITC

ITC's e-Choupal initiative is a prime example of leveraging technology for rural development. e-Choupal provides farmers with access to real-time information on weather, market prices, and best agricultural practices through internet kiosks in villages. This digital platform empowers farmers to make informed decisions, enhancing their productivity and incomes. The initiative has reached millions of farmers across thousands of villages, illustrating the potential of digital inclusion in transforming rural economies.

Conclusion

Initiatives that make a difference are driven by a shared vision of a better world and the determination to turn that vision into reality. From education and healthcare to environmental conservation and social justice, these efforts demonstrate the profound impact that collective action can have. By supporting and participating in such initiatives, each of us can contribute to creating a more just, equitable, and sustainable world.

As we reflect on these initiatives, let us be inspired to take our own steps beyond boundaries, harnessing our unique abilities and resources to make a positive difference in the lives of others. Together, we can build a legacy of social impact that transcends generations.

Chapter 27

PERSONAL STORIES OF COMMUNITY LEADERS

In every community, there are individuals whose actions and dedication to social causes inspire others to pursue change. These community leaders, through their unwavering commitment and passion, break boundaries and transform lives. Their stories are a testament to the power of individual action in creating collective impact. This chapter delves into the personal stories of such leaders, exploring their motivations, challenges, and the lasting legacies they have built.

1. Rani Patel: Champion of Women's Education

Rani Patel grew up in a rural village in India where education for girls was not prioritized. Despite the societal norms, Rani's parents supported her education, allowing her to become the first girl in her village to complete high school. However, the path was not easy. Rani faced immense pressure to marry early and abandon her studies. Determined to change the narrative for other girls in her community, she founded the "Udaan Foundation," an organization dedicated to promoting girls' education.

Through Udaan, Rani has provided scholarships, built schools, and conducted awareness programs about the importance of educating girls. Her work has led to a significant increase in the number of girls attending school in her village and neighboring areas. Rani's story is a powerful reminder that one person's courage and determination can create opportunities for many.

2. Carlos Martinez: Advocate for Urban Green Spaces

Carlos Martinez, a landscape architect from Brazil, saw firsthand how urbanization was erasing green spaces in cities, affecting the quality of life for residents. He decided to dedicate his career to preserving and creating green spaces in urban areas. Carlos founded "Green Cities Initiative," an organization that works with local governments and communities to design and implement sustainable urban parks.

One of Carlos' most notable projects was transforming a neglected, crime-ridden area into a vibrant community park in São Paulo. The project involved not only physical changes but also community engagement, fostering a sense of ownership and pride among residents. Carlos' work has demonstrated the critical role of green spaces in enhancing urban living and has inspired similar initiatives worldwide.

3. Aisha Mohammed: Health Crusader in Conflict Zones

Aisha Mohammed, a nurse from Nigeria, has spent over two decades providing medical care in conflict zones. Her journey began when she volunteered with an international medical organization during the civil unrest in her country. Witnessing the dire need for healthcare in war-torn areas, Aisha decided to focus her efforts on bringing medical aid to those most affected by conflict.

Aisha founded "Hope on Wheels," a mobile clinic service that delivers medical care to remote and dangerous regions. Despite the risks, she and her team travel to areas with little to no healthcare infrastructure, providing essential services such as vaccinations, maternal care, and emergency treatments. Aisha's bravery and dedication have saved countless lives and brought hope to communities ravaged by conflict.

4. David Chen: Environmental Protector

David Chen, an environmental scientist from Taiwan, grew concerned about the rapid decline of biodiversity in his country. Determined to make a difference, he left his corporate job to focus on conservation. David established "Biodiversity Guardians," an NGO dedicated to protecting endangered species and their habitats.

One of David's significant achievements was the successful conservation of the Formosan black bear, an endangered species native to Taiwan. Through research, advocacy, and community engagement, Biodiversity Guardians has not only increased the bear population but also raised awareness about the importance of biodiversity. David's efforts have highlighted the critical link between environmental health and human well-being.

5.   Leila Hassan: Social Entrepreneur Empowering Youth

Leila Hassan, a social entrepreneur from Kenya, witnessed the challenges faced by young people in her community, including unemployment and lack of opportunities. Believing in the potential of youth to drive change, Leila founded "Youth for Change," an organization that provides training, mentorship, and resources to empower young people to start their own businesses and social enterprises.

Through Youth for Change, Leila has helped thousands of young people develop skills, create jobs, and become active contributors to their communities. Her innovative programs have included everything from tech incubators to agricultural cooperatives, showcasing the diverse potential of youth-led initiatives. Leila's work has demonstrated the transformative power of investing in the next generation.

6.   Anand Kumar: Education Reformer

Anand Kumar, a mathematician from Bihar, India, grew up facing financial challenges that often hindered his educational pursuits. Despite these obstacles, he managed to secure a place at the prestigious University of Cambridge, only to forgo the opportunity due to his family's financial constraints. This experience ignited his passion for education reform, particularly for underprivileged students.

Anand founded the "Super 30" program, which selects 30 talented but economically disadvantaged students each year and provides them with free coaching, food, and accommodation to help them crack the Indian Institute of Technology (IIT) entrance exam. His innovative teaching methods and dedication have resulted in a high success rate, with many of his students securing spots at IITs and transforming their lives and communities. Anand's story is a testament to the power of education in breaking the cycle of poverty.

7.   Jeroo Billimoria: Social Entrepreneur for Children's Rights

Jeroo Billimoria, from Mumbai, India, has dedicated her life to addressing the needs of marginalized children. Witnessing the struggles of street children in Mumbai, she was inspired to create systems that ensure their rights and well-being. Jeroo founded "Childline India

Foundation," a 24-hour emergency phone service for children in distress.

Childline has become a lifeline for millions of children across India, providing immediate assistance and long-term support. Jeroo's approach integrates government agencies, NGOs, and community groups to create a robust network of child protection. Her work has not only saved countless children from abuse and exploitation but also empowered them to advocate for their rights. Jeroo's impact extends globally through her other initiatives, which focus on financial inclusion and social entrepreneurship.

Conclusion
The stories of Rani, Carlos, Aisha, David, Leila, Anand, and Jeroo illustrate the profound impact that individuals can have on their communities. These leaders, through their vision, resilience, and dedication, have broken boundaries and created lasting social change. Their personal journeys serve as a source of inspiration, reminding us that anyone can make a difference, no matter the challenges they face. As we continue our exploration of social impact, may these stories encourage us to take action and contribute to the betterment of our own communities.

Chapter 28

THE JOY OF GIVING BACK

The act of giving back is a profound and transformative experience that transcends individual gain, fostering a sense of community, purpose, and interconnectedness. It is an embodiment of altruism, reflecting a deep understanding that our true wealth lies in the impact we create in the lives of others. This chapter delves into the joy of giving back, exploring its significance, the myriad ways it can be practiced, and the profound effects it has on both the giver and the receiver.

The Essence of Giving Back

Giving back is rooted in the philosophy that we are all part of a larger whole, and our actions ripple out to affect the collective well-being. It is not confined to grand gestures or financial donations; it encompasses small acts of kindness, volunteering time, sharing knowledge, and even extending emotional support. The essence of giving back is about recognizing our shared humanity and contributing to the betterment of society.

The Psychological and Emotional Benefits

Numerous studies have highlighted the psychological and emotional benefits of giving. Engaging in acts of generosity activates regions of the brain associated with pleasure, social connection, and trust, often referred to as the "helper's high." This phenomenon leads to increased levels of happiness, reduced stress, and a greater sense of purpose. When we give, we not only improve the lives of others but also enhance our own well-being.

Building Stronger Communities

Giving back fosters stronger, more resilient communities. It creates networks of support that can be relied upon in times of need. Whether through community service, local initiatives, or supporting charitable organizations, these acts of generosity build a sense of solidarity and mutual respect. They remind us that we are not alone and that, together, we can overcome challenges and create positive change.

Personal Stories of Impact

Consider the story of Anand Kumar, the founder of Super 30, an educational program in India that trains underprivileged students for the Indian Institutes of Technology (IIT) entrance exams. Anand's commitment to giving back has transformed the lives of countless students, offering them a pathway out of poverty and into a future filled with possibilities. His journey exemplifies how one person's dedication can ignite hope and inspire others to give back.

Another powerful example is the global movement initiated by Malala Yousafzai, the youngest Nobel Prize laureate, who advocates for girls' education worldwide. Despite facing immense adversity, Malala's unwavering commitment to this cause has mobilized millions and highlighted the transformative power of education. Her story is a testament to how giving back can drive systemic change and uplift entire communities.

Ways to Give Back

There are countless ways to incorporate giving back into our daily lives:

Volunteering Time: Whether at local shelters, schools, or community centers, offering your time can make a significant impact.

Sharing Knowledge: Mentoring, teaching, or providing professional advice can empower others and help them achieve their goals.

Financial Contributions: Donating to causes you care about, whether through direct contributions or crowdfunding platforms.

Acts of Kindness: Simple gestures, like helping a neighbor, supporting a friend in need, or participating in community clean-ups, can create a ripple effect of positivity.

Advocacy: Championing causes and raising awareness about social issues can lead to broader societal changes.

Overcoming Barriers to Giving

Despite its benefits, some may find it challenging to give back due to time constraints, financial limitations, or a sense of inadequacy. Overcoming these barriers involves recognizing that giving back is not about the magnitude of the contribution but the intention behind it. Every effort, no matter how small, is valuable and contributes to the greater good.

Conclusion

The joy of giving back lies in the fulfillment and connection it brings. It reminds us of our shared humanity and the power we hold to effect change. As we navigate our personal and professional journeys, integrating acts of generosity into our lives enriches our experiences and strengthens the social fabric of our communities. In giving back, we find true joy and a deeper sense of purpose, transcending boundaries to create a lasting, positive impact on the world.

By embracing the joy of giving back, we not only enhance our own lives but also contribute to the collective well-being, paving the way for a brighter, more inclusive future.

Chapter 29

HOW PHILANTHROPY TRANSFORMS LIVES

In a world where social inequities and challenges abound, philanthropy stands as a beacon of hope, transforming lives and creating lasting impact. Philanthropy, derived from the Greek words "philos" (loving) and "anthropos" (human), literally means "love for humanity." It encompasses the desire to promote the welfare of others, often expressed through generous donations of money, time, or resources to causes that address societal needs. This chapter delves into the transformative power of philanthropy, exploring its multifaceted impact on individuals, communities, and the philanthropists themselves.

The Ripple Effect of Philanthropy

Philanthropy has a ripple effect, where the initial act of giving sets off a chain of positive events. This ripple effect extends far beyond the immediate beneficiaries, fostering a culture of generosity and collective responsibility.

Individual Impact: At the individual level, philanthropy can be life-changing. For those in need, philanthropic efforts can provide access to essential resources such as food, shelter, healthcare, and education. For instance, scholarships funded by philanthropic donations can enable underprivileged students to pursue higher education, breaking the cycle of poverty and opening doors to new opportunities.

Community Development: Philanthropy also plays a crucial role in community development. By investing in local projects such as schools, hospitals, and community centers, philanthropists can help build resilient and self-sufficient communities. These investments not only improve the quality of life for residents but also foster a sense of community pride and ownership.

Global Reach: On a global scale, philanthropy can address pressing issues such as climate change, global health crises, and humanitarian disasters. Organizations like the Bill & Melinda Gates Foundation have demonstrated how strategic philanthropic efforts can tackle global challenges, funding initiatives that range from eradicating diseases to promoting sustainable development.

Stories of Transformation

The true power of philanthropy is best illustrated through the stories of those whose lives have been transformed.

Malala Yousafzai: Malala's story is a testament to the transformative power of education and the impact of philanthropic support. After surviving a Taliban attack for advocating girls' education, Malala received global support through various philanthropic initiatives. Today, the Malala Fund works to ensure every girl has access to 12 years of free, safe, and quality education, transforming the lives of countless girls around the world.

The Impact of Microfinance: The Grameen Bank, founded by Nobel Laureate Muhammad Yunus, revolutionized the concept of microfinance. By providing small loans to impoverished individuals, particularly women, the bank empowered them to start their own businesses and lift themselves out of poverty. The success stories of these micro-entrepreneurs highlight how a relatively small act of philanthropy can have a profound impact on individual lives and entire communities.

The Philanthropist's Journey

Philanthropy not only transforms the lives of beneficiaries but also enriches the lives of the philanthropists themselves. The journey of giving can lead to personal growth, fulfillment, and a deeper understanding of the world.

Personal Fulfillment: Many philanthropists report a sense of fulfillment and purpose that comes from knowing they are making a difference. The act of giving can provide a profound sense of satisfaction, enhancing the giver's well-being and happiness.

Legacy Building: Philanthropy allows individuals to leave a lasting legacy. By supporting causes they are passionate about, philanthropists can ensure their values and contributions endure beyond their lifetimes. This legacy of giving can inspire future generations to continue the cycle of philanthropy.

Broadened Perspectives: Engaging in philanthropy often exposes individuals to different cultures, perspectives, and challenges. This broadened worldview can foster empathy, understanding, and a deeper appreciation for the interconnectedness of humanity.

The Role of Strategic Philanthropy

While the desire to help others is at the heart of philanthropy, strategic philanthropy focuses on creating sustainable and scalable solutions to social problems. This approach involves careful planning, research, and collaboration to maximize impact.

Evidence-Based Giving: Strategic philanthropists use data and research to identify the most effective ways to address social issues. By funding evidence-based programs and initiatives, they ensure their contributions have the greatest possible impact.

Collaboration and Partnership: Effective philanthropy often involves collaboration with other organizations, governments, and communities. By working together, philanthropic entities can pool resources, share expertise, and create comprehensive solutions to complex problems.

Long-Term Commitment: Strategic philanthropy recognizes that lasting change often requires long-term commitment. Sustainable impact is achieved through consistent support, ongoing evaluation, and the flexibility to adapt strategies as needed.

Philanthropy as a Catalyst for Change

Ultimately, philanthropy serves as a catalyst for change, empowering individuals and communities to overcome challenges and achieve their full potential. It embodies the principles of compassion, generosity, and collective responsibility, reminding us of our shared humanity.

As we reflect on the transformative power of philanthropy, it is essential to recognize that everyone has the potential to make a difference. Whether through financial contributions, volunteer work, or simply spreading awareness, each act of giving contributes to a larger movement of positive change. By embracing the spirit of philanthropy, we can create a world where everyone has the opportunity to thrive, transcending boundaries and building a brighter future for all.

Chapter 30

INSPIRING PHILANTHROPIC EFFORTS

Introduction

Philanthropy, derived from the Greek words "philos" (loving) and "anthropos" (humankind), encapsulates the spirit of benevolence and compassion towards humanity. It transcends the act of giving, embodying a profound commitment to fostering societal well-being and addressing the root causes of suffering and inequality. In "Beyond Boundaries: A Guide to Personal, Professional, Social, and Spiritual Growth," understanding the transformative power of philanthropy is pivotal to achieving social impact. This chapter delves into inspiring philanthropic efforts that have significantly contributed to societal advancement, demonstrating how individuals and organizations can make a lasting difference.

The Essence of Philanthropy

At its core, philanthropy is about more than just financial contributions; it is about investing time, energy, and resources to create a positive change. True philanthropists are driven by a deep sense of empathy and a desire to address social injustices. Their efforts often extend beyond immediate relief, aiming for sustainable development and systemic change.

Case Study 1: Bill and Melinda Gates Foundation

The Bill and Melinda Gates Foundation stands as a beacon of modern philanthropy. Established in 2000, the foundation has committed billions of dollars to various global causes, including health, education, and poverty alleviation. One of their most notable initiatives is the fight against malaria. By funding research and supporting the distribution of mosquito nets and vaccines, the foundation has significantly reduced malaria-related deaths worldwide. The Gates Foundation's approach to philanthropy highlights the importance of strategic planning, measurable outcomes, and partnerships with local communities and governments.

Case Study 2: Malala Fund

Founded by Malala Yousafzai, the youngest Nobel Prize laureate, the Malala Fund champions the cause of girls' education. After surviving a Taliban attack for advocating for her right to education, Malala transformed her personal tragedy into a global movement. The Malala Fund invests in local education advocates in regions where girls face significant barriers to education. By amplifying the voices of these advocates and supporting their efforts, the fund is working towards a world where every girl can learn and lead.

The Ripple Effect of Grassroots Movements

While large foundations have the resources to implement wide-reaching programs, grassroots movements often drive change from the ground up. These community-led efforts are crucial in addressing localized issues with culturally relevant solutions. An inspiring example is the Barefoot College in India. Founded by Bunker Roy, this organization trains women from rural communities to become solar engineers. Known as "Solar Mamas," these women bring sustainable energy solutions to their villages, promoting environmental sustainability and economic empowerment.

Corporate Philanthropy: A New Paradigm

Corporate philanthropy has evolved from sporadic donations to strategic, integrated initiatives that align with a company's core values and business goals. Patagonia, an outdoor clothing company, exemplifies this shift. Committed to environmental conservation, Patagonia donates 1% of its sales to environmental causes and supports grassroots activists through its Action Works platform. The company's approach underscores the potential of businesses to drive positive change while maintaining profitability.

The Role of Technology in Philanthropy

Technology has revolutionized philanthropic efforts by enhancing transparency, efficiency, and reach. Crowdfunding platforms like GoFundMe and GlobalGiving have democratized philanthropy, allowing individuals to contribute to causes they care about regardless of their financial capacity. Social media has also played a pivotal role in raising awareness and mobilizing support for various causes. The ALS Ice

Bucket Challenge is a prime example, where a viral campaign raised over $115 million for amyotrophic lateral sclerosis (ALS) research.

Personal Philanthropy: Making a Difference

While the efforts of large organizations and influential individuals are commendable, personal philanthropy is equally impactful. Acts of kindness, volunteering, and community service contribute significantly to societal well-being. Every individual has the power to effect change within their means. Establishing a culture of giving in everyday life, whether through mentoring, donating, or supporting local initiatives, creates a ripple effect that strengthens communities.

Case Study 3: The Tony Elumelu Foundation

The Tony Elumelu Foundation, established by Nigerian entrepreneur Tony Elumelu, focuses on empowering African entrepreneurs. Through its flagship program, the Tony Elumelu Entrepreneurship Program (TEEP), the foundation offers training, mentorship, and funding to thousands of startups across Africa. This initiative aims to drive economic growth and job creation by supporting innovative business ideas. The foundation's approach exemplifies how targeted support for entrepreneurship can catalyze regional development and uplift entire communities.

Case Study 4: Operation Smile

Operation Smile is an international medical charity that provides free cleft palate and cleft lip surgeries to children and adults in underdeveloped countries. Founded in 1982 by Dr. William Magee and Kathleen Magee, the organization has performed over 300,000 surgeries to date. Operation Smile's model of volunteerism, collaboration with local medical professionals, and provision of follow-up care illustrates the impact of combining medical expertise with compassionate outreach. Their work not only restores smiles but also transforms lives by improving the quality of life and enabling individuals to thrive in their communities.

Case Study 5: The Giving Pledge

The Giving Pledge is a commitment by some of the world's wealthiest individuals and families to give away the majority of their wealth to address society's most pressing problems. Launched in 2010 by Warren

Buffett and Bill and Melinda Gates, the pledge encourages billionaires to publicly commit to giving away at least half of their wealth during their lifetime or in their will. Signatories of the pledge include notable figures like Elon Musk and Richard Branson. The Giving Pledge highlights the influence of wealthy individuals in fostering a culture of philanthropy and leveraging their resources to tackle global challenges.

Conclusion: A Call to Action
Philanthropy is a powerful tool for social transformation. The inspiring efforts highlighted in this chapter demonstrate that anyone, regardless of their position or resources, can contribute to making the world a better place. By embracing a philanthropic mindset, we move beyond personal and professional boundaries to create a lasting social impact. As you reflect on these stories, consider how you can incorporate philanthropic efforts into your life. Remember, true growth and fulfillment come from not just achieving personal and professional success, but also from contributing to the greater good. Together, we can build a more just, equitable, and compassionate world.

THINKING BEYOND BORDERS

Introduction

In an increasingly interconnected world, the notion of borders is not limited to geographical lines. These borders often encompass cultural, social, economic, and ideological divides. The concept of "Thinking Beyond Borders" is about transcending these limitations to embrace a more inclusive, global perspective. This chapter explores how expanding our thinking beyond conventional boundaries can drive social impact and foster innovation, understanding, and collaboration across diverse communities.

The Limits of Conventional Thinking

Traditional boundaries, whether physical, cultural, or ideological, often restrict our ability to see beyond immediate contexts. These borders can be:

Geographical: National borders or regional divides that limit our view to local perspectives.

Cultural: Norms and values that shape how we perceive other cultures, potentially leading to stereotyping or ethnocentrism.

Social: Class, race, gender, and socioeconomic barriers that create disparities and hinder social cohesion.

Ideological: Fixed belief systems that prevent open-mindedness and acceptance of differing viewpoints.

These borders often perpetuate misunderstanding, conflict, and missed opportunities for collaboration. To make a meaningful social impact, it is essential to challenge and move beyond these limitations.

Expanding Horizons: The Power of a Global Perspective

Cultural Exchange and Empathy: Engaging with different cultures through travel, education, and dialogue fosters empathy and mutual respect. By understanding diverse cultural practices and values, individuals and organizations can build bridges and collaborate more effectively.

Global Problem-Solving: Addressing global challenges such as climate change, poverty, and health crises requires cross-border cooperation. Thinking beyond national interests and working collectively can lead to innovative solutions and more effective responses to these issues.

Diverse Perspectives and Innovation: Bringing together people from various backgrounds and disciplines can spark creativity and innovation. Diverse teams are better equipped to approach problems from multiple angles, leading to more robust and novel solutions.

Technology and Connectivity: The digital age has diminished physical boundaries, allowing for instant communication and collaboration across the globe. Leveraging technology to connect with others and share knowledge can accelerate progress and foster global networks.

Case Studies of Thinking beyond Borders

The Global Village Project: This initiative supports refugee girls in gaining education and integrating into new communities. By bridging cultural and educational gaps, the project empowers these young women to achieve their potential and contribute to society.

The One World Trade Center: Designed with input from architects and engineers worldwide, this iconic structure represents a collective effort to rebuild and symbolize resilience after the 9/11 attacks. It stands as a testament to how international collaboration can lead to remarkable achievements.

Global Health Initiatives: Organizations like the World Health Organization (WHO) and Médecins Sans Frontières (Doctors Without Borders) exemplify how global cooperation in healthcare can address health crises and improve outcomes for communities worldwide.

Practical Steps to Think Beyond Borders

Educate Yourself: Seek knowledge about different cultures, global issues, and diverse perspectives. Engage with literature, media, and experiences that broaden your understanding.

Foster Inclusivity: Create environments where diverse voices are heard and valued. Encourage participation from people with different backgrounds and viewpoints.

Collaborate Globally: Participate in or support international projects and initiatives. Use digital tools to connect with people across the world and collaborate on shared goals.

Challenge Assumptions: Regularly question your own biases and assumptions. Embrace the discomfort that comes with confronting your own limitations and seek to understand opposing viewpoints.

Conclusion

Thinking beyond borders is not merely an idealistic notion but a practical approach to addressing the complexities of the modern world. By transcending conventional limitations, we can foster greater understanding, drive social progress, and contribute to a more inclusive and equitable global community. Embracing this mindset allows us to break down barriers, innovate, and collaborate in ways that create meaningful and lasting social impact.

In essence, thinking beyond borders is about recognizing that our shared humanity binds us more closely than any physical or ideological divides. It challenges us to extend our reach, broaden our perspectives, and work together to build a better world for everyone.

Chapter 32

GLOBAL CITIZENSHIP AND THE ROLE OF GLOBAL CITIZENS

Introduction

In an increasingly interconnected world, the concept of global citizenship has emerged as a vital framework for addressing the complex challenges that transcend national borders. Global citizenship extends beyond mere national identity, emphasizing a shared responsibility toward humanity and the planet. This chapter explores the essence of global citizenship, its significance in contemporary society, and the transformative role that global citizens play in fostering social impact.

Defining Global Citizenship

Global citizenship is defined as an awareness and appreciation of one's identity as part of the global community. It involves recognizing and acting upon the interconnectedness of individuals and nations, understanding global issues, and taking proactive steps to contribute positively to the world. Unlike traditional citizenship, which is bound by national or regional borders, global citizenship encompasses a broader perspective, emphasizing collective well-being and mutual respect among diverse cultures and societies.

The Importance of Global Citizenship

Addressing Global Challenges: Global issues such as climate change, poverty, and inequality require coordinated efforts across nations. Global citizens are pivotal in advocating for sustainable practices, supporting humanitarian initiatives, and promoting equitable solutions that benefit all of humanity.

Promoting Peace and Security: In a world fraught with conflict and tensions, global citizens play a crucial role in fostering dialogue, understanding, and cooperation among different cultures and nations. By embracing diversity and encouraging peaceful resolutions, global citizens contribute to a more stable and harmonious world.

Enhancing Cultural Understanding: Global citizenship involves recognizing and valuing cultural differences while promoting cross-cultural exchanges. This understanding enriches societies, dismantles stereotypes, and builds bridges between communities, fostering a more inclusive and tolerant global society.

Encouraging Social Justice: Global citizens are advocates for human rights and social justice. They work towards eliminating discrimination, addressing systemic inequalities, and ensuring that marginalized voices are heard and valued. Their efforts contribute to creating a more just and equitable world.

The Role of Global Citizens

Advocacy and Activism: Global citizens engage in advocacy and activism to address pressing global issues. They support international organizations, participate in campaigns, and use their voices to raise awareness about critical topics such as environmental sustainability, human rights, and education.

Education and Awareness: By educating themselves and others about global issues, global citizens contribute to a more informed and proactive society. They share knowledge, challenge misinformation, and promote critical thinking, thereby empowering individuals to make informed decisions and take meaningful actions.

Volunteering and Service: Many global citizens dedicate their time and resources to volunteer work and service projects that address local and global needs. Whether through international development programs, disaster relief efforts, or community service, their contributions make a tangible difference in improving the lives of others.

Sustainable Living: Global citizens adopt and promote sustainable practices in their daily lives. This includes reducing their carbon footprint, supporting ethical businesses, and advocating for policies that protect the environment. Their commitment to sustainability helps mitigate the impact of human activities on the planet.

Building Networks and Partnerships: Global citizens often collaborate with individuals, organizations, and governments across borders to achieve common goals. By building networks and forming partnerships, they amplify their impact and create synergistic solutions to global challenges.

Challenges and Opportunities

Navigating Cultural Differences: While global citizenship promotes cultural understanding, it also requires navigating and respecting diverse cultural norms and practices. Global citizens must approach intercultural interactions with sensitivity and openness to avoid misunderstandings and conflicts.

Addressing Inequality: Global citizenship can sometimes perpetuate inequalities if not practiced inclusively. It is essential for global citizens to address power imbalances and ensure that their efforts do not exacerbate existing disparities but rather contribute to equitable solutions.

Balancing Local and Global Priorities: Global citizens must balance their local responsibilities with global aspirations. Ensuring that local actions align with global goals requires careful consideration and strategic planning to achieve meaningful impact at both levels.

Conclusion

Global citizenship represents a profound shift in how we perceive our roles and responsibilities in a globalized world. It challenges us to transcend national boundaries and embrace a shared commitment to improving the human condition and protecting the planet. By embodying the principles of global citizenship—advocacy, education, service, sustainable living, and collaboration—individuals can drive significant social impact and contribute to a more just, peaceful, and interconnected world.

Embracing global citizenship not only enriches our understanding of the world but also empowers us to make a difference that resonates across borders. As we navigate the complexities of our global society, let us remember that our collective actions have the power to shape a brighter future for generations to come.

Chapter 33

STORIES OF INDIVIDUALS MAKING A GLOBAL IMPACT

Introduction

India has a rich tapestry of individuals, whose contributions have resonated far beyond its borders, impacting the global stage with their pioneering work, vision, and commitment to positive change. In this chapter, we will delve into the stories of five remarkable Indian figures whose influence has made a significant mark globally.

1. Dr. A.P.J. Abdul Kalam: The People's President

Dr. A.P.J. Abdul Kalam, known as the "Missile Man of India," played a pivotal role in India's space and missile programs. His leadership as the chief architect of the Indian missile program and his contributions to the development of the Indian space program earned him global recognition. Beyond his scientific achievements, Kalam's tenure as the President of India and his work as a mentor and educator made him a beloved figure worldwide.

Kalam's story is a testament to how dedication to one's field, combined with a commitment to education and inspiring others, can create a legacy that transcends national boundaries. His emphasis on innovation and youth empowerment continues to inspire future generations globally.

2. Satyendra Nath Bose: Pioneer of Bose-Einstein Statistics

Satyendra Nath Bose, a physicist from India, made groundbreaking contributions to the field of quantum mechanics. His work on Bose-Einstein statistics laid the foundation for the development of quantum theory and the study of particles known as bosons, which has had a profound impact on modern physics.

Bose's collaboration with Albert Einstein led to the formulation of Bose-Einstein Condensate, a state of matter that has become fundamental in quantum research. His contributions highlight the global nature of scientific progress and the significant role that Indian scholars have played in shaping modern science.

3. Verghese Kurien: The Father of the White Revolution

Verghese Kurien was the driving force behind India's White Revolution, which transformed the country into one of the largest producers of milk and dairy products globally. By pioneering the cooperative movement in dairy farming, Kurien not only revolutionized India's dairy industry but also empowered millions of rural farmers.

His work with the National Dairy Development Board (NDDB) and the Amul cooperative led to significant economic and social changes, impacting global dairy practices and inspiring similar movements in other countries. Kurien's legacy underscores the potential of grassroots innovation to effect global change.

4. Sundar Pichai: Leading Innovation in Technology

Sundar Pichai, the CEO of Alphabet Inc. (Google's parent company), is a prominent example of Indian talent making a global impact in the tech industry. Under his leadership, Google has continued to innovate and expand its influence in technology, including advancements in artificial intelligence and cloud computing.

Pichai's journey from his modest beginnings in India to the helm of one of the world's most influential technology companies highlights the global opportunities available to those with vision and determination. His story inspires many, showing how talent and innovation can break through international boundaries and drive technological progress.

5. Mother Teresa: A Beacon of Compassion

Mother Teresa dedicated her life to serving the poorest of the poor in Kolkata, India. Founding the Missionaries of Charity, she provided care for the sick, dying, and destitute, embodying compassion and selflessness. Her work earned her the Nobel Peace Prize and widespread recognition, not just for her humanitarian efforts but for her profound impact on the perception of charity and service.

Mother Teresa's life teaches us that even the smallest acts of kindness can create significant ripples of change. Her story emphasizes the importance of compassion and the ability of one person to make a difference in the lives of thousands.

6. Greta Thunberg: The Voice of Climate Activism

Greta Thunberg, a Swedish teenager, catalyzed a global movement for climate action through her "Fridays for Future" strikes. Her impassioned speeches and advocacy have mobilized millions of young people around the world to demand urgent action against climate change. Thunberg's influence extends to global leaders and policymakers, pushing climate issues to the forefront of international discussions.

Conclusion

These stories illustrate the profound global impact that individuals from India have made in various fields. Their achievements not only highlight the diverse talents emerging from India but also emphasize the universal nature of innovation, compassion, and leadership.

As we reflect on these narratives, we recognize that breaking through boundaries—whether in science, technology, literature, or social justice—can lead to transformative global contributions. These individuals inspire us to pursue our passions, embrace challenges, and strive for a world where impactful change knows no borders.

PART IV
Spiritual Enlightenment Beyond Boundaries

Chapter 34

UNDERSTANDING SPIRITUALITY

Introduction

In the journey of life, spirituality often serves as a guiding star, offering meaning, purpose, and a deeper understanding of our place in the universe. Spirituality is not confined to religious practices or doctrines; it encompasses a broad spectrum of beliefs and experiences that connect us to something greater than us. In this chapter, we will explore the essence of spirituality, its different facets, and how understanding it can enrich our lives.

Defining Spirituality

Spirituality is a complex and multi-dimensional concept. At its core, it involves a quest for meaning and connection beyond the material and physical aspects of existence. Unlike religion, which is often organized and doctrinal, spirituality is a personal and individualized experience. It might involve:

Connection to a Higher Power or Universal Force: For many, spirituality involves a sense of connection to a higher power, the universe, or a divine entity. This connection can manifest through prayer, meditation, or contemplation.

Search for Meaning and Purpose: Spirituality encourages individuals to explore existential questions and seek a sense of purpose and meaning in life.

Inner Peace and Self-Discovery: It often involves a journey inward, promoting self-awareness, inner peace, and personal growth.

Compassion and Service: Spirituality frequently manifests through acts of kindness, compassion, and service to others.

Historical and Cultural Perspectives

Throughout history and across cultures, spirituality has taken various forms. Ancient philosophies, such as those found in Hinduism,

Buddhism, Taoism, and indigenous traditions, have long emphasized spiritual practices and beliefs. Each tradition offers unique insights into the nature of existence and the path to spiritual enlightenment:

Hinduism: Emphasizes the pursuit of Moksha (liberation from the cycle of birth and rebirth) through practices like meditation, yoga, and devotion.

Buddhism: Focuses on achieving Nirvana (enlightenment) through the Four Noble Truths and the Eightfold Path, emphasizing mindfulness and ethical living.

Taoism: Advocates for living in harmony with the Tao (the fundamental nature of the universe) through simplicity, humility, and compassion.

Indigenous Traditions: Often center around a deep connection to nature and ancestral spirits, emphasizing the sacredness of the Earth and the interrelationship of all beings.

Spirituality in Modern Times

In contemporary society, spirituality has evolved to encompass a diverse range of practices and beliefs. While traditional religious institutions remain significant, many people now explore spirituality outside of formal religions. This modern approach includes:

Mindfulness and Meditation: Techniques for cultivating awareness, reducing stress, and enhancing personal well-being.

Personal Development and Self-Help: Exploring spirituality through personal growth, self-improvement, and psychological insights.

Holistic Health: Integrating spiritual practices with physical and mental health, such as through yoga and alternative therapies.

Interfaith and Non-religious Spirituality: Embracing a blend of various spiritual practices or finding meaning without adhering to a specific religious framework.

The Benefits of Understanding Spirituality

Understanding spirituality can offer numerous benefits, including:

Enhanced Well-being: Spiritual practices can reduce stress, increase resilience, and promote overall mental and emotional health.

Greater Purpose and Meaning: Exploring spiritual beliefs can provide a sense of direction and purpose in life.

Improved Relationships: Spirituality often fosters compassion, empathy, and a sense of interconnectedness with others.

Personal Growth: Engaging with spiritual practices can lead to deeper self-awareness and personal development.

Practical Steps to Explore Spirituality

If you're interested in exploring spirituality, consider the following steps:

Reflect on Your Beliefs: Take time to contemplate your own beliefs and values. What gives your life meaning?

Explore Various Practices: Experiment with different spiritual practices such as meditation, prayer, or reading spiritual texts.

Seek Guidance: Engage with spiritual teachers, mentors, or communities that resonate with you.

Practice Mindfulness: Incorporate mindfulness techniques into your daily routine to enhance self-awareness and inner peace.

Be Open-Minded: Approach spirituality with an open mind and be willing to explore new ideas and perspectives.

Conclusion

Understanding spirituality is a deeply personal journey that can enrich our lives in profound ways. It invites us to explore the deeper dimensions of our existence, connect with something greater than ourselves, and find meaning and purpose in our everyday experiences. By embracing spirituality, we open ourselves to a more fulfilling and enlightened way of living, transcending boundaries and discovering our true selves.

Chapter 35

PATHS TO SPIRITUAL ENLIGHTENMENT

Introduction

Spiritual enlightenment represents the culmination of a journey that transcends the boundaries of conventional understanding. It is a profound state of awareness and understanding that reveals the interconnectedness of all existence and the true nature of self. This chapter delves into the various paths to spiritual enlightenment, each offering unique perspectives and practices to help individuals navigate their personal journey towards greater spiritual realization.

The Quest for Spiritual Enlightenment

Spiritual enlightenment is often described as an awakening—a sudden or gradual realization of the deeper truths about existence, consciousness, and the self. This quest for enlightenment can be approached through multiple paths, each resonating with different aspects of human experience. Understanding these paths can help individuals find the one that aligns best with their personal beliefs, experiences, and spiritual aspirations.

1. Path of Knowledge (Jnana Yoga)

The Path of Knowledge, or Jnana Yoga, is rooted in the pursuit of wisdom and understanding. It involves deep study of sacred texts, contemplation, and meditation on fundamental questions about existence and the nature of reality. Key aspects of this path include:

Self-Inquiry: Engaging in self-inquiry involves asking questions such as "Who am I?" and "What is the nature of my consciousness?" This practice encourages individuals to look beyond the ego and the superficial self to uncover their true essence.

Study of Scriptures: Many spiritual traditions emphasize the study of sacred texts and philosophies, such as the Bhagavad Gita, the Upanishads, or the works of prominent philosophers and sages. These texts provide insights into the nature of the self and the universe.

Contemplation and Reflection: Regular contemplation and reflection on spiritual teachings help integrate knowledge into daily life and foster a deeper understanding of spiritual truths.

2. Path of Devotion (Bhakti Yoga)

The Path of Devotion, or Bhakti Yoga, centers on cultivating a deep, loving relationship with the divine. This path is characterized by:

Devotional Practices: Engaging in practices such as prayer, chanting, and worship helps to cultivate a personal connection with the divine. Acts of devotion foster a sense of surrender and love towards a higher power.

Surrender and Trust: Bhakti Yoga emphasizes surrendering to the divine will and trusting in the guidance and grace of a higher power. This surrender is not about passivity but about aligning one's actions and intentions with divine principles.

Community and Service: Participating in spiritual communities and engaging in acts of selfless service (seva) are integral to Bhakti Yoga. These activities help individuals express their devotion through compassionate actions.

3. Path of Meditation (Raja Yoga)

The Path of Meditation, or Raja Yoga, focuses on the practice of meditation and mental discipline to achieve spiritual insight. Key components include:

Meditative Practices: Raja Yoga involves various meditation techniques aimed at calming the mind and achieving inner stillness. Techniques such as mindfulness meditation, concentration, and visualization are employed.

Eight Limbs of Yoga: Raja Yoga, as outlined by Patanjali in the Yoga Sutras, includes the Eight Limbs (Ashtanga) that provide a comprehensive approach to spiritual practice. These limbs cover ethical principles, self-discipline, physical postures, breath control, concentration, meditation, and self-realization.

Self-Mastery: This path emphasizes the importance of self-mastery and control over the mind and emotions. Achieving mental clarity and inner peace is seen as essential for spiritual progress.

4. Path of Action (Karma Yoga)

The Path of Action, or Karma Yoga, is centered on selfless action and service to others. This path teaches that spiritual growth is achieved through:

Selfless Service: Performing actions without attachment to the results or personal gain is a key principle of Karma Yoga. This selflessness helps individuals transcend ego and cultivate compassion.

Mindful Engagement: Engaging in daily activities with mindfulness and dedication can be a form of spiritual practice. Every action becomes an opportunity to practice non-attachment and serve others.

Equanimity: Karma Yoga encourages maintaining equanimity and detachment from the fruits of one's actions. By focusing on the process rather than the outcomes, individuals can achieve a sense of inner balance.

5. Path of Integration (Integral Yoga)

Integral Yoga, as developed by Sri Aurobindo, seeks to integrate various aspects of the self—physical, mental, and spiritual—into a unified whole. This path involves:

Holistic Development: Emphasizing the development of the entire being, including physical health, mental clarity, and spiritual awareness. Integral Yoga encourages a balanced approach to personal growth.

Transformation of Consciousness: This path focuses on the transformation of individual consciousness and the integration of higher spiritual experiences into everyday life.

Divine Presence: Recognizing the divine presence in all aspects of life and working towards manifesting higher spiritual qualities in all actions.

Conclusion

The paths to spiritual enlightenment are as diverse as the individuals who walk them. Each path offers unique practices and insights, yet they all converge on the ultimate goal of spiritual awakening and self-realization. Whether through knowledge, devotion, meditation, action, or integration, the journey towards enlightenment is a deeply personal and transformative experience. By exploring these various paths, individuals can find their unique way to transcending boundaries and achieving spiritual fulfillment.

Chapter 36

PERSONAL JOURNEYS OF SPIRITUAL AWAKENING

Introduction

In the tapestry of human existence, spiritual awakening represents a profound transformation—one that transcends ordinary understanding and touches the very essence of our being. This chapter delves into the personal journeys of spiritual awakening, exploring how individuals across cultures and backgrounds have navigated their paths to spiritual enlightenment. By examining these diverse experiences, we gain insight into the universal quest for meaning and the boundless potential of the human spirit.

The Essence of Spiritual Awakening

Spiritual awakening is often described as a profound shift in consciousness, where individuals experience a heightened sense of awareness and connection to something greater than themselves. It is a journey of rediscovering one's true self, breaking free from the limitations of the ego, and embracing a more expansive and interconnected perspective on life.

At its core, spiritual awakening involves several key elements:

Self-Discovery: Uncovering one's authentic self beyond societal roles and expectations.

Transcendence: Moving beyond the confines of individual identity to connect with a higher consciousness or universal truth.

Inner Peace: Experiencing a profound sense of inner calm and contentment, irrespective of external circumstances.

Unity: Recognizing and embracing the interconnectedness of all life forms and the universe.

Personal Journeys: Stories of Transformation

1. The Path of Self-Realization: Siddhartha Gautama

One of the most renowned accounts of spiritual awakening is that of Siddhartha Gautama, who later became the Buddha. Born into royalty, Siddhartha lived a life of luxury until he encountered the realities of human suffering—old age, sickness, and death. These encounters sparked a profound inner quest for understanding and liberation.

Leaving behind his privileged life, Siddhartha embarked on a rigorous path of asceticism and meditation. His journey led him to enlightenment under the Bodhi tree, where he attained profound insights into the nature of suffering and the path to liberation. Siddhartha's awakening emphasizes the importance of self-inquiry, discipline, and the transformative power of direct experience.

2. The Spiritual Journey of Rumi

Jalaluddin Rumi, a 13th-century Persian poet and mystic, offers another profound example of spiritual awakening. Rumi's journey was marked by a deep and transformative encounter with the divine, catalyzed by the loss of his beloved mentor, Shams of Tabriz.

Rumi's poetry reflects his mystical experiences and his understanding of divine love. His verses capture the essence of spiritual awakening as a process of surrendering the ego and embracing the boundless love of the divine. Rumi's teachings invite us to dissolve the barriers between ourselves and the divine, seeking a direct and intimate connection with the sacred.

3. Modern Insights: Eckhart Tolle

In contemporary times, Eckhart Tolle's journey exemplifies the transformative power of spiritual awakening. Struggling with depression and anxiety, Tolle experienced a profound shift in consciousness during a moment of intense despair. This awakening led him to a deeper understanding of the present moment and the nature of the mind.

Tolle's teachings, particularly in his book "The Power of Now," emphasize the importance of living in the present and recognizing the illusory nature of the ego. His personal journey highlights the accessibility of spiritual awakening in everyday life and the profound impact it can have on one's sense of peace and fulfillment.

Common Themes in Personal Journeys

Despite the diversity of experiences, certain themes recur in the personal journeys of spiritual awakening:

Crisis as Catalyst: Many individuals experience a profound shift during periods of personal crisis or suffering, which acts as a catalyst for deeper self-exploration and awakening.

Seeking Beyond Conventional Boundaries: Spiritual awakening often involves moving beyond conventional beliefs and societal expectations, seeking a more authentic and expansive understanding of oneself and the universe.

The Role of Practice: Meditation, contemplation, and other spiritual practices play a crucial role in facilitating and deepening the awakening process.

Conclusion

The personal journeys of spiritual awakening reveal a rich tapestry of experiences that highlight the universal quest for meaning and connection. Whether through ancient traditions or modern insights, these stories offer valuable lessons on the nature of consciousness, the importance of self-discovery, and the transformative power of spiritual realization. As we explore these journeys, we are reminded that spiritual awakening is not confined by boundaries but is an open, expansive journey available to all who seek it.

Chapter 37

MEDITATION AND MINDFULNESS

Introduction

In a world characterized by constant motion and distraction, the pursuit of spiritual enlightenment often feels elusive. Yet, within the chaos lies a profound opportunity for personal growth and inner peace. This chapter explores the transformative power of meditation and mindfulness—practices that not only anchor us in the present moment but also pave the way for deeper self-awareness and spiritual awakening.

Understanding Meditation

1. Definition and Origins

Meditation is a practice rooted in ancient traditions, aimed at focusing the mind and achieving a state of inner calm and clarity. Its origins span various cultures and religions, including Hinduism, Buddhism, Taoism, and even early Christian mysticism. Despite their differences, these traditions share a common goal: to transcend ordinary consciousness and experience a higher state of awareness.

2. The Science behind Meditation

Modern science has begun to validate the benefits of meditation, revealing its impact on the brain and overall well-being. Studies using neuroimaging techniques have shown that meditation can enhance areas of the brain associated with emotional regulation, attention, and self-awareness. Additionally, regular practice has been linked to reduced stress, improved immune function, and increased resilience.

The Practice of Mindfulness

1. Defining Mindfulness

Mindfulness is a form of meditation that emphasizes being fully present in the moment. It involves paying attention to one's thoughts, feelings, and sensations without judgment. This practice encourages a non-reactive awareness, allowing individuals to observe their experiences without being overwhelmed by them.

2. Techniques for Cultivating Mindfulness

Several techniques can help cultivate mindfulness:

Breathing Exercises: Focus on the breath, noticing its natural rhythm. When the mind wanders, gently bring attention back to the breath.

Body Scan: Systematically focus on different parts of the body, noticing sensations without judgment.

Mindful Walking: Pay attention to the physical sensations of walking, including the feeling of the ground underfoot and the movement of the body.

The Benefits of Meditation and Mindfulness

1. Emotional Balance

Both practices contribute to emotional stability by promoting a greater awareness of one's emotional landscape. This awareness helps individuals recognize and manage their reactions, leading to more balanced emotional responses.

2. Stress Reduction

Meditation and mindfulness have been shown to significantly reduce stress levels. By promoting relaxation and reducing the body's stress response, these practices help individuals cope more effectively with life's challenges.

3. Enhanced Self-Awareness

Through regular practice, individuals gain insight into their thought patterns and behavioral habits. This self-awareness fosters personal growth and facilitates a deeper understanding of one's true nature.

4. Improved Relationships

Mindfulness and meditation can enhance interpersonal relationships by cultivating empathy, patience, and understanding. Being more present in interactions allows for more meaningful and compassionate connections with others.

Integrating Meditation and Mindfulness into Daily Life

1. Establishing a Routine

Consistency is key to reaping the benefits of meditation and mindfulness. Setting aside a specific time each day for practice, even if only for a few minutes, can create a habit that becomes an integral part of daily life.

2. Applying Mindfulness in Daily Activities

Mindfulness can be practiced beyond formal meditation sessions. Incorporating mindfulness into everyday activities—such as eating, driving, or even washing dishes—can help maintain a sense of presence throughout the day.

3. Overcoming Challenges

Practitioners may encounter challenges such as a wandering mind or difficulty finding time. It's important to approach these challenges with patience and persistence. Remember that the goal is not perfection but rather the ongoing journey toward greater awareness.

Conclusion

Meditation and mindfulness are powerful tools for spiritual enlightenment and personal growth. By fostering a deeper connection to the present moment and enhancing self-awareness, these practices offer a pathway to inner peace and profound transformation. Embracing meditation and mindfulness can lead to a richer, more fulfilling life, transcending the boundaries of everyday existence and opening doors to spiritual awakening.

Chapter 38

TECHNIQUES AND PRACTICES

Introduction
In the pursuit of spiritual enlightenment, the journey is deeply personal and profoundly transformative. While each individual's path is unique, certain techniques and practices can serve as powerful tools in fostering spiritual growth. This chapter explores various techniques and practices that can help individuals transcend boundaries and achieve a higher state of spiritual awareness.

1. Meditation
Meditation is a cornerstone of spiritual practice. It involves focusing the mind and eliminating distractions to achieve a state of deep relaxation and heightened awareness.

Techniques:
Mindfulness Meditation: This practice involves paying attention to the present moment without judgment. It helps cultivate awareness of thoughts and feelings, allowing for greater self-understanding and inner peace.

Loving-Kindness Meditation (Metta): This technique focuses on developing feelings of compassion and love towards oneself and others. It involves repeating phrases such as "May I/you be happy, may I/you be healthy," fostering a sense of connection and empathy.

Transcendental Meditation: This form of meditation uses a mantra to transcend ordinary thought and access a deeper state of consciousness. The mantra is repeated silently to quiet the mind and achieve a state of restful awareness.

2. Mindfulness
Mindfulness is the practice of being fully present and engaged in the current moment. It involves observing one's thoughts, feelings, and surroundings without judgment.

Practices:

Body Scan: This technique involves focusing attention on different parts of the body, from head to toe, to increase bodily awareness and relaxation.

Mindful Eating: Paying close attention to the taste, texture, and sensation of food can transform eating into a mindful practice, promoting gratitude and awareness.

Mindful Walking: Walking slowly and attentively, paying attention to each step and the sensations of movement, helps integrate mindfulness into daily activities.

3. Yoga

Yoga is a practice that combines physical postures, breath control, and meditation to promote physical and spiritual well-being.

Techniques:

Hatha Yoga: Focuses on physical postures and breath control to prepare the body and mind for meditation.

Kundalini Yoga: Aims to awaken the dormant spiritual energy within through a combination of postures, breathwork, and chanting.

Bhakti Yoga: Centers around devotion and love for the divine, often expressed through prayer, chanting, and rituals.

4. Journaling

Journaling can be a powerful tool for self-reflection and spiritual growth. It involves writing down thoughts, feelings, and insights to gain clarity and insight into one's spiritual journey.

Techniques:

Gratitude Journaling: Regularly writing down things one is grateful for helps cultivate a positive mindset and enhances spiritual well-being.

Reflective Journaling: Writing about personal experiences, challenges, and insights can provide a deeper understanding of oneself and one's spiritual path.

Intuitive Journaling: Allowing the pen to move freely and write without a predetermined direction can help uncover hidden thoughts and feelings.

5. Contemplative Reading

Reading spiritual texts and literature can provide guidance and inspiration on the path to enlightenment. Contemplative reading involves engaging deeply with these texts and reflecting on their meanings.

Techniques:

Sacred Texts: Studying texts such as the Bhagavad Gita, Tao Te Ching, or the Bible can offer profound insights and wisdom.

Inspirational Quotes: Reflecting on quotes from spiritual leaders and thinkers can provide motivation and guidance.

Philosophical Works: Exploring philosophical writings on topics such as consciousness, existence, and the nature of reality can deepen spiritual understanding.

6. Rituals and Ceremonies

Rituals and ceremonies can create sacred space and time for spiritual practice, helping individuals connect with higher realms and honor their spiritual journey.

Practices:

Daily Rituals: Incorporating practices such as lighting candles, offering prayers, or performing specific ceremonies into daily life can foster a sense of devotion and mindfulness.

Seasonal Ceremonies: Participating in ceremonies that align with natural cycles and seasons can enhance spiritual connection and harmony with the natural world.

Personal Ceremonies: Creating personalized rituals to mark significant life events or transitions can provide a sense of closure and renewal.

Conclusion

The techniques and practices outlined in this chapter serve as pathways to spiritual enlightenment, each offering unique benefits and opportunities for growth. By integrating these practices into daily life, individuals can transcend boundaries, deepen their spiritual understanding, and embark on a transformative journey towards higher consciousness.

Chapter 39

CASE STUDIES OF INDIVIDUALS WHO ACHIEVED PEACE THROUGH MEDITATION

Introduction

In the pursuit of spiritual enlightenment, meditation has long been a beacon of hope and transformation. This chapter explores the journeys of individuals who have achieved profound peace through meditation, illustrating how this practice can transcend personal limitations and lead to a more harmonious existence. Through these case studies, we will examine the diverse ways in which meditation has facilitated inner tranquility and personal growth.

Case Study 1: Swami Vivekananda

Background: Swami Vivekananda, born Narendranath Datta, was a prominent Indian monk and disciple of Ramakrishna Paramahamsa. Before his spiritual awakening, he was a brilliant student with a deep interest in philosophy and spirituality.

Journey: Swami Vivekananda's path to meditation began with his studies under Ramakrishna, who introduced him to profound spiritual practices and the concept of meditation as a means to self-realization. Vivekananda's journey included extensive meditation and contemplation, which he integrated into his teachings.

Outcome: Swami Vivekananda's meditation practice profoundly influenced his philosophy and public speaking. His teachings on Vedanta and the power of meditation played a crucial role in the revival of Hindu spirituality and inspired many across the world. His speech at the Parliament of the World's Religions in Chicago brought global recognition to Indian spiritual traditions and meditation practices.

Analysis: Swami Vivekananda's life demonstrates how meditation can be a powerful tool for spiritual awakening and global influence. His emphasis on meditation and self-realization continues to inspire and guide individuals seeking a deeper understanding of themselves and their place in the world.

Case Study 2: Maharishi Ramana

Background: Maharishi Ramana Maharshi, born Venkataraman Iyer, was a revered Indian sage known for his teachings on self-enquiry and meditation. He lived a largely solitary life in the Arunachala hills, where he dedicated himself to spiritual practice.

Journey: Maharishi Ramana's meditation practice was centered around the technique of self-enquiry (Atma Vichara), which involves questioning the nature of the self and seeking the true Self. His approach was marked by a deep sense of inner peace and detachment from worldly concerns.

Outcome: Maharishi Ramana's teachings and meditation practice had a profound impact on those who sought his guidance. His approach to meditation and self-enquiry led many to experience a state of inner stillness and spiritual realization. His legacy continues through the ongoing study and practice of his teachings.

Analysis: Maharishi Ramana's case highlights meditation's role in achieving a state of profound inner peace and self-realization. His method of self-enquiry offers a path to understanding the nature of the self and attaining spiritual enlightenment.

Case Study 3: Sri Aurobindo

Background: Sri Aurobindo, originally named Aurobindo Ghose, was an Indian philosopher, poet, and spiritual leader who significantly contributed to the modern understanding of meditation and spirituality. His early life included an extensive education and involvement in the Indian independence movement.

Journey: Sri Aurobindo's spiritual journey led him to develop a comprehensive approach to meditation and spiritual practice. He founded the Sri Aurobindo Ashram and developed Integral Yoga, a practice that integrates meditation with personal and collective transformation.

Outcome: Sri Aurobindo's Integral Yoga emphasized the union of the divine with the material world and sought to transform human consciousness. His meditation practices and teachings have inspired many to pursue a holistic approach to spiritual growth and societal progress. His work continues to influence modern spiritual and philosophical thought.

Analysis: Sri Aurobindo's experience underscores the integration of meditation with broader spiritual and societal goals. His approach to Integral Yoga highlights meditation's potential for personal transformation and collective evolution, demonstrating its role in shaping both individual and societal progress.

Case Study 4: Swami Sivananda

Background: Swami Sivananda Saraswati was a renowned Indian yogi and spiritual teacher known for his extensive contributions to yoga and meditation. Before his spiritual awakening, Swami Sivananda worked as a medical doctor, but he felt an inner calling towards spiritual practice.

Journey: After leaving his medical career, Swami Sivananda dedicated himself to meditation and the study of Vedanta. He founded the Divine Life Society in Rishikesh, where he taught various forms of meditation and yoga. His teachings emphasized the importance of meditation for achieving inner peace and self-realization.

Outcome: Swami Sivananda's meditation practices and teachings had a profound impact on his followers and the broader spiritual community. His emphasis on meditation as a means to attain spiritual enlightenment and mental serenity has inspired countless individuals worldwide. His teachings continue to influence modern yoga and meditation practices.

Analysis: Swami Sivananda's journey demonstrates the transformative power of meditation in shifting one's life path from a conventional career to spiritual fulfillment. His legacy highlights meditation's role in achieving inner peace and spiritual growth, impacting both personal development and global spiritual practices.

Case Study 5: Osho (Rajneesh)

Background: Osho, also known as Rajneesh, was an Indian mystic and spiritual teacher known for his innovative approach to meditation and personal growth. Before gaining prominence, Osho was a philosophy professor with a deep interest in spiritual practices.

Journey: Osho developed a unique approach to meditation, combining traditional techniques with contemporary methods. He founded the Rajneesh Movement and established an ashram in Pune, where he introduced dynamic meditation, a practice designed to release repressed emotions and achieve inner peace.

Outcome: Osho's meditation techniques attracted a global following and were credited with helping many individuals achieve emotional release and spiritual insight. His teachings emphasized living in the present moment and embracing one's true self, contributing to a broader understanding of meditation's role in personal transformation.

Analysis: Osho's case illustrates how innovative approaches to meditation can address modern psychological and emotional challenges. His contributions highlight meditation's potential for personal liberation and the development of new techniques to enhance spiritual and emotional well-being.

Case Study 6: The Corporate Executive's Transformation

Background: Sarah Mitchell, a successful corporate executive, was known for her high-stress lifestyle and relentless pursuit of career goals. Despite her achievements, she struggled with anxiety and dissatisfaction.

Journey: Faced with mounting stress and health issues, Sarah turned to meditation as a last resort. Initially skeptical, she began with guided mindfulness sessions to manage her anxiety. Over time, she incorporated a daily practice of transcendental meditation.

Outcome: Sarah reported a significant decrease in stress levels and an improved sense of well-being. Her newfound calmness enhanced her decision-making skills and work performance. Additionally, she found greater fulfillment in her personal life, attributing these positive changes to her meditation practice.

Analysis: Sarah's case highlights meditation's potential to reduce stress and improve mental clarity. By integrating meditation into her daily routine, she was able to cultivate inner peace and balance, which positively impacted both her professional and personal life.

Case Study 7: The Overcoming of Grief

Background: James Carter, a retired military officer, faced profound grief following the loss of his spouse. Struggling with depression and feelings of isolation, James sought a way to cope with his overwhelming emotions.

Journey: Encouraged by a friend, James began practicing Vipassana meditation, a technique focused on self-awareness and equanimity. His initial sessions were challenging, but he persevered, attending meditation retreats to deepen his practice.

Outcome: Through Vipassana meditation, James experienced a gradual but profound shift in his emotional state. He reported a greater acceptance of his grief and an increased sense of inner peace. Meditation provided him with tools to navigate his emotions and find solace in the midst of his loss.

Analysis: James's experience underscores meditation's capacity to help individuals process grief and find peace amidst emotional turmoil. The practice allowed him to gain perspective and acceptance, demonstrating meditation's role in emotional healing.

Case Study 8: The Entrepreneur's awakening

Background: Maria Gomez, an ambitious entrepreneur, faced burnout due to her relentless work ethic and constant pursuit of success. Her health deteriorated, and she experienced frequent bouts of exhaustion.

Journey: Maria decided to explore meditation as a means to restore balance in her life. She engaged in Zen meditation, which emphasized mindfulness and simplicity. She committed to daily sessions and integrated mindfulness into her business practices.

Outcome: Maria noticed a marked improvement in her overall well-being. Her ability to manage stress improved, leading to better decision-making and a more balanced approach to her work. Meditation also fostered a deeper sense of purpose and connection to her work beyond financial success.

Analysis: Maria's case illustrates how meditation can enhance not only personal well-being but also professional effectiveness. By incorporating mindfulness into her entrepreneurial journey, she achieved a more sustainable and fulfilling approach to success.

Case Study 9: The Artist's Creative Revival

Background: David Johnson, a talented artist, struggled with creative blocks and a lack of inspiration. His frustration with his artistic stagnation led to feelings of inadequacy and self-doubt.

Journey: Seeking to rekindle his creativity, David turned to meditation practices that focused on cultivating inner stillness and clarity. He practiced loving-kindness meditation to foster a positive mindset and open himself to creative possibilities.

Outcome: David experienced a resurgence in his creative abilities and a renewed passion for his art. Meditation helped him overcome self-imposed limitations and connect with a deeper sense of inspiration. His artwork became more expressive and resonant with his inner experiences.

Analysis: David's experience highlights meditation's role in unlocking creative potential and overcoming artistic barriers. By fostering a state of inner calm and openness, meditation facilitated a reconnection with his creative essence.

Conclusion

These case studies demonstrate that meditation can lead to profound personal transformation and inner peace. Whether managing stress, navigating grief, achieving professional balance, or unlocking creativity, individuals from various walks of life have found solace and growth through meditation. The common thread among these cases is the ability of meditation to foster a deeper understanding of oneself and a more harmonious existence. As we explore these journeys, we are reminded of meditation's transformative potential in the quest for spiritual enlightenment and personal growth.

Chapter 40

THE POWER OF PURPOSE

Introduction

In the pursuit of spiritual enlightenment, understanding the power of purpose is fundamental. Purpose is more than a mere goal or aspiration; it is the driving force behind our actions and decisions, a beacon that guides us through the complexities of life. This chapter explores how purpose shapes our spiritual journey, influences our growth, and ultimately helps us transcend the boundaries of our existence.

The Essence of Purpose

Purpose is the core of our being. It is the reason we wake up every morning with enthusiasm and commitment. This intrinsic drive is what gives meaning to our daily activities and long-term ambitions. From a spiritual perspective, purpose aligns our actions with our core values and beliefs, leading us towards self-realization and fulfillment.

Purpose as a Spiritual Compass

Purpose acts as a spiritual compass, directing us toward our true north. It provides clarity amidst confusion and helps us navigate through life's challenges. When we have a clear sense of purpose, we are more likely to stay focused on what truly matters, making decisions that are in harmony with our spiritual values.

Purpose and Personal Growth

Purpose fuels personal growth by encouraging us to overcome obstacles and expand our horizons. It drives us to seek out new experiences, develop our skills, and improve ourselves. Through this process, we not only grow as individuals but also align more closely with our spiritual goals, creating a path of continuous self-improvement.

Purpose and Inner Fulfillment

Inner fulfillment is deeply connected to our sense of purpose. When we engage in activities that resonate with our core beliefs and passions, we experience a profound sense of satisfaction and contentment. This alignment between our actions and purpose fosters a sense of inner peace and joy, which is essential for spiritual enlightenment.

The Role of Passion in Purpose

Passion is a key element in discovering and living our purpose. It ignites our enthusiasm and motivates us to pursue our goals with vigor. Passionate engagement in activities that align with our purpose enhances our sense of fulfillment and contributes to our overall well-being.

Purpose and Resilience

A strong sense of purpose cultivates resilience, enabling us to face adversity with strength and grace. When we are driven by a clear purpose, we are better equipped to handle challenges, maintain a positive outlook, and persevere in the face of difficulties. This resilience is crucial for maintaining our spiritual journey and achieving enlightenment.

Living with Purpose

Living with purpose involves more than just setting goals; it requires integrating purpose into every aspect of our lives. It means aligning our actions, relationships, and choices with our deeper values and spiritual beliefs. Here are some ways to live a purpose-driven life:

Self-Reflection and Awareness

Regular self-reflection helps us gain clarity about our purpose. By examining our values, passions, and aspirations, we can better understand what drives us and how to align our actions with our purpose. Mindfulness practices, journaling, and meditation can be valuable tools in this process.

Setting Meaningful Goals

Setting goals that are in alignment with our purpose ensures that we are working towards what truly matters to us. These goals should reflect our values and contribute to our overall spiritual growth. By pursuing meaningful objectives, we reinforce our sense of purpose and enhance our journey towards enlightenment.

Cultivating Purposeful Relationships

Our relationships play a significant role in our spiritual growth. Surrounding ourselves with individuals who share our values and support our purpose fosters an environment that nurtures our personal and spiritual development. Meaningful connections enhance our sense of belonging and contribute to our overall sense of purpose.

Purpose and Transcendence

Ultimately, purpose is a gateway to transcendence. By living in alignment with our deepest values and spiritual beliefs, we transcend the limitations of our ego and connect with a higher sense of meaning. This transcendence is a profound aspect of spiritual enlightenment, leading us to a deeper understanding of ourselves and our place in the universe.

Conclusion

The power of purpose is a transformative force in our spiritual journey. It guides us, fuels our growth, and brings fulfillment to our lives. By embracing our purpose, living with intention, and aligning our actions with our core values, we move closer to spiritual enlightenment and transcend the boundaries of our existence. As we continue to explore and embrace our purpose, we unlock the potential for profound spiritual growth and fulfillment.

Chapter 41

FINDING AND PURSUING YOUR LIFE'S PURPOSE

Introduction

In the journey of personal, professional, and social growth, discovering and pursuing your life's purpose stands as a fundamental pillar of spiritual enlightenment. Your life's purpose is more than just a goal or ambition; it is the core reason for your existence, the essence of your being, and the driving force behind your actions and decisions. This chapter will explore the process of finding your life's purpose and the steps necessary to pursue it with determination and clarity.

1. Understanding Life's Purpose

Life's purpose is often described as a profound sense of meaning and direction that aligns with your core values and passions. It transcends daily tasks and immediate goals, providing a sense of fulfillment and satisfaction that comes from knowing you are contributing to something greater than yourself.

Defining Your Purpose

To define your purpose, start by reflecting on the following:

Passions and Interests: What activities or causes ignite your enthusiasm? Identifying what excites you can offer clues to your purpose.

Values: What principles are fundamental to your identity? Understanding your core values helps in aligning your purpose with what matters most to you.

Strengths and Talents: What are you naturally good at? Leveraging your strengths in areas that resonate with you can lead to discovering your purpose.

The Role of Self-Reflection

Self-reflection is key to understanding your purpose. Engage in regular practices such as journaling, meditation, or contemplative walks to explore your thoughts and feelings. Ask yourself:

What legacy do I want to leave behind?
What activities make me lose track of time?
When do I feel most alive and connected?

2. Aligning with Your Purpose

Once you have a sense of your purpose, the next step is aligning your daily life and decisions with it. This involves making conscious choices that reflect your purpose and integrating it into your personal and professional spheres.

Setting Purposeful Goals

Establish goals that are directly related to your purpose. These goals should challenge you while being achievable, pushing you to grow in alignment with your purpose. For example, if your purpose involves helping others, setting goals related to community service or mentorship can be fulfilling.

Creating a Purpose-Driven Routine

Incorporate activities that support your purpose into your daily routine. Whether it's dedicating time to a passion project, engaging in meaningful work, or connecting with like-minded individuals, consistent actions will reinforce your commitment to your purpose.

3. Overcoming Obstacles

Pursuing your purpose is not without challenges. Common obstacles include self-doubt, societal pressures, and fear of failure. Addressing these challenges with resilience and adaptability is crucial.

Managing Self-Doubt

Self-doubt can undermine your pursuit of purpose. Combat it by focusing on past successes, seeking feedback from trusted mentors, and maintaining a positive mindset. Remember that doubt is a natural part of growth and can be managed through perseverance and self-compassion.

Navigating Societal Expectations

Societal norms and expectations can sometimes conflict with your personal purpose. To navigate these pressures, stay true to your values and seek a balance that respects both your purpose and social responsibilities. Surround yourself with supportive individuals who encourage your journey.

Embracing Failure as Growth

Failure is an inevitable part of pursuing a purpose. Instead of viewing it as a setback, see it as a learning opportunity. Analyze what went wrong, adjust your strategies, and continue moving forward with renewed determination.

4. Sustaining Your Purpose

Maintaining a strong connection to your purpose over time requires continuous effort and reflection.

Periodic Reassessment

Regularly reassess your purpose and goals to ensure they remain aligned with your evolving values and aspirations. Life experiences and personal growth can lead to shifts in purpose, and staying adaptable is key.

Celebrating Achievements

Acknowledge and celebrate milestones along your journey. Recognizing your achievements reinforces your commitment and provides motivation to continue pursuing your purpose.

Conclusion

Finding and pursuing your life's purpose is a transformative journey that leads to spiritual enlightenment and personal fulfillment. By understanding and aligning with your purpose, overcoming obstacles, and sustaining your commitment, you can live a life that is deeply meaningful and rewarding. Embrace the journey with courage and dedication, knowing that your pursuit of purpose contributes to your spiritual growth and the greater good of those around you.

Chapter 42

INSPIRATIONAL STORIES OF PURPOSE DRIVEN LIVES

Introduction

In the journey of spiritual enlightenment, purpose-driven lives stand out as beacons of light, guiding others toward their own paths of fulfillment. These stories embody the essence of living with intention and conviction, transforming not only their own lives but also the lives of those around them. This chapter explores the lives of remarkable individuals who have pursued their deeper callings with unwavering dedication, illustrating how their purpose-driven actions transcend personal boundaries and inspire global change.

1. Mahatma Gandhi: The Path of Nonviolence

Mahatma Gandhi's life is a profound testament to the power of purpose-driven living. Born in India, Gandhi's early experiences and education in law led him to South Africa, where he first encountered racial discrimination. This personal injustice ignited his purpose: to fight for civil rights and justice through nonviolent resistance. His philosophy of Satyagraha (truth force) became the cornerstone of his activism, influencing not only India's struggle for independence but also civil rights movements worldwide. Gandhi's purpose was not merely to achieve political freedom but to inspire a universal respect for human dignity and equality. His life reminds us that purpose, when combined with steadfast principles, can effect profound societal change.

2. Mother Teresa: Serving the Destitute

Mother Teresa, born as Anjezë Gonxhe Bojaxhiu in Albania, dedicated her life to serving the poorest of the poor in Kolkata, India. Her purpose emerged from a deep sense of compassion and a calling to serve those abandoned by society. Founding the Missionaries of Charity, she and her order provided care for the dying, lepers, and orphans. Despite facing numerous challenges, including limited resources and severe poverty, her unwavering commitment to alleviating human suffering exemplifies a life driven by purpose. Mother Teresa's legacy continues to inspire countless individuals to find their own ways to serve and uplift those in need.

3. Nelson Mandela: Champion of Reconciliation

Nelson Mandela's journey from anti-apartheid activist to President of South Africa is a powerful example of a purpose-driven life shaped by resilience and forgiveness. Imprisoned for 27 years, Mandela's purpose remained steadfast: to end racial segregation and promote reconciliation. Upon his release, he chose to lead with a spirit of unity rather than revenge, guiding South Africa through a peaceful transition to democracy. Mandela's life illustrates that a deep sense of purpose can guide one through immense personal sacrifice and contribute to healing a nation deeply divided.

4. Jane Goodall: Guardian of the Wild

Jane Goodall's groundbreaking work with chimpanzees has redefined our understanding of primates and our place in the animal kingdom. Her purpose began with a simple love for animals and a desire to study them in their natural habitat. Through her extensive research, Goodall not only advanced scientific knowledge but also became a leading advocate for environmental conservation and animal welfare. Her life's work emphasizes how following one's passion can lead to significant contributions in both science and advocacy, inspiring others to protect and respect the natural world.

5. Malala Yousafzai: Advocate for Girls' Education

Malala Yousafzai's courageous stand for girls' education in the face of life-threatening opposition from the Taliban embodies a remarkable purpose-driven life. After surviving an assassination attempt, Malala's resolve only strengthened, and she continued her advocacy on a global scale. Her work through the Malala Fund aims to ensure every girl has the opportunity to receive 12 years of quality education. Malala's story serves as a powerful reminder that a clear purpose—driven by a deep sense of justice and equality—can ignite global movements and inspire change despite daunting obstacles.

6. Viktor Frankl: The Search for Meaning

Viktor Frankl, a Holocaust survivor and psychiatrist, discovered a profound purpose amidst the horrors of concentration camps. His experiences led him to develop logotherapy, a psychological approach centered on finding meaning in life, even in the face of suffering. Frankl's seminal work, Man's Search for Meaning, explores how individuals can transcend their circumstances by identifying a deeper purpose. His life and teachings highlight that purpose can emerge from the most challenging experiences, guiding people toward resilience and personal fulfillment.

7. Wangari Maathai: Environmental and Women's Rights Activist

Wangari Maathai, a Kenyan environmentalist, founded the Green Belt Movement, an environmental organization focused on tree planting, environmental conservation, and women's empowerment. Maathai's purpose was driven by her deep connection to nature and a commitment to improving the lives of women and rural communities in Kenya. Her efforts not only led to the planting of over 50 million trees but also inspired global environmental and social movements. Maathai's legacy demonstrates how a clear purpose can address both environmental and social issues simultaneously.

8. Desmond Tutu: Voice for Peace and Justice

Archbishop Desmond Tutu, a prominent South African cleric and human rights activist, dedicated his life to fighting apartheid and advocating for peace and reconciliation. Tutu's purpose was rooted in his faith and commitment to justice, and he played a crucial role in the Truth and Reconciliation Commission, which sought to heal the wounds of a divided nation. His work in promoting forgiveness and human rights exemplifies how a purpose-driven life can contribute to national healing and global justice.

9. Fred Rogers: Champion of Childhood Education

Fred Rogers, creator of the beloved television show Mister Rogers' Neighborhood, had a profound purpose to educate and nurture the emotional and moral development of children. Rogers's innovative approach to children's programming focused on kindness, empathy, and self-worth. His dedication to creating a safe and understanding space for children to explore their feelings and learn about the world underscores the impact of purpose-driven work on shaping future generations.

10. Tim Berners-Lee: Inventor of the World Wide Web

Tim Berners-Lee, a British computer scientist, invented the World Wide Web with the purpose of improving information sharing and communication across the globe. His vision was to create a universal platform that could enhance collaboration and access to knowledge. The Web revolutionized how we interact, learn, and work, demonstrating how a single individual's purpose-driven innovation can transform global society and connectivity.

11. Oprah Winfrey: Advocate for Personal Empowerment

Oprah Winfrey, media mogul and philanthropist, has dedicated her life to empowering individuals and communities through education, personal growth, and philanthropy. Her purpose-driven approach is evident in her work with The Oprah Winfrey Foundation and Oprah's Book Club, which aim to uplift and inspire. Winfrey's journey from overcoming personal adversity to becoming a global influencer highlights the power of purpose in creating opportunities and fostering positive change.

12. Elon Musk: Visionary Entrepreneur

Elon Musk, the founder of Tesla and SpaceX, has pursued ambitious goals with the purpose of advancing technology and sustainability. His commitment to reducing climate change through electric vehicles and exploring space for future human habitation reflects a forward-thinking purpose. Musk's endeavors illustrate how a vision driven by purpose can lead to groundbreaking innovations that address global challenges and push the boundaries of what is possible.

13. Baba Amte: Advocate for Leprosy Patients

Baba Amte, an Indian social worker, devoted his life to the care and rehabilitation of leprosy patients. His purpose emerged from his deep empathy for the marginalized and his commitment to transforming their lives. Amte founded Anandwan, a self-sustained community for leprosy patients, providing them with medical care, education, and vocational training. His work not only improved the lives of countless individuals but also changed societal attitudes towards leprosy. Amte's legacy underscores the impact of living with purpose and compassion.

14. Dr. Abdul Kalam: Visionary Scientist and President

Dr. A.P.J. Abdul Kalam, known as the "Missile Man of India," dedicated his life to advancing India's space and defense technologies. His purpose was driven by a vision of transforming India into a self-reliant and technologically advanced nation. As a scientist, educator, and later as President of India, Kalam inspired millions with his commitment to education and nation-building. His life exemplifies how a clear purpose in science and leadership can foster national progress and inspire future generations.

15. Satyendra Nath Bose: Pioneer in Theoretical Physics

Satyendra Nath Bose, an eminent physicist, made significant contributions to theoretical physics, particularly in quantum mechanics. His collaboration with Albert Einstein led to the development of Bose-Einstein statistics and the discovery of Bose-Einstein condensates. Bose's dedication to scientific research and his pursuit of knowledge reflect a purpose-driven life in advancing scientific understanding. His contributions continue to influence modern physics and demonstrate the impact of purpose in the realm of scientific inquiry.

16. M.S. Swaminathan: Champion of Agricultural Reform

Dr. M.S. Swaminathan, an agricultural scientist and nutritionist, has been a key figure in India's Green Revolution. His purpose was to improve food security and agricultural productivity in India through innovative farming techniques and research. Swaminathan's efforts in developing high-yielding crop varieties and promoting sustainable farming practices have significantly enhanced agricultural sustainability and food security. His work highlights the role of purpose in addressing critical issues such as hunger and rural development.

17. Sunita Williams: Space Explorer

Sunita Williams, an Indian-American astronaut, has made notable contributions to space exploration with NASA. Her purpose-driven career is marked by her participation in multiple space missions, including a long-duration stay aboard the International Space Station. Williams's achievements in space research and her commitment to advancing space exploration reflect a life driven by a vision of expanding human knowledge and capabilities beyond Earth. Her journey inspires future generations to pursue their passions and contribute to scientific advancement.

18. Dr. Verghese Kurien: Father of the White Revolution

Dr. Verghese Kurien, known as the architect of India's White Revolution, transformed India's dairy industry through the cooperative movement. His purpose was to improve the livelihoods of rural dairy farmers and ensure milk production for the nation. Kurien's establishment of the National Dairy Development Board and the Amul cooperative revolutionized dairy farming in India, providing economic benefits to millions of farmers and ensuring a stable supply of dairy products. His work exemplifies how purpose-driven innovation can address both economic and social challenges.

19. Sudha Murthy: Philanthropist and Author

Sudha Murthy, chairperson of the Infosys Foundation, has dedicated her life to philanthropy and social work. Her purpose is to support education, healthcare, and rural development in India. Through her foundation, Murthy has funded numerous initiatives, including schools, hospitals, and infrastructure projects, benefiting underserved communities across the country. Her contributions extend beyond her philanthropic efforts to her work as an author and advocate for social issues, highlighting how purpose-driven actions can create lasting positive change.

20. J.R.D. Tata: Industrialist and Philanthropist

J.R.D. Tata, the founder of Tata Group, was a pioneering industrialist and philanthropist whose purpose was to build and support India's industrial and social infrastructure. His vision included not only business success but also contributions to education, healthcare, and social welfare. Tata's establishment of institutions like Tata Institute of Fundamental Research and Tata Memorial Hospital reflects his commitment to enhancing India's scientific and medical capabilities. His life's work demonstrates how a purpose-driven approach to business can lead to broader societal advancements.

Conclusion

These stories of purpose-driven live shighlight the diverse ways in which individuals can impact society through their dedication and vision. From advancing science and technology to improving social welfare and environmental sustainability, their achievements serve as powerful examples of how purpose can guide and inspire transformative action.

Chapter 43

SUMMARIZE KEY INSIGHTS

As we draw to a close on this transformative journey through "Beyond Boundaries: A Guide to Personal, Professional, Social, and Spiritual Growth," it is vital to distill the essence of the insights we have gathered. Each chapter has been a stepping stone, guiding us toward a more enriched and fulfilling existence. Here, we summarize the key insights that form the foundation of our growth beyond boundaries.

Personal Growth

1. **Embrace Change:** Change is the only constant. Embracing change, rather than resisting it, allows us to adapt and thrive in an ever-evolving world. We learned that change is not a threat but an opportunity for growth and innovation.

2. **Self-Awareness:** The journey of personal growth begins with self-awareness. Understanding our strengths, weaknesses, values, and motivations enables us to make informed decisions and align our actions with our true selves.

3. **Resilience and Perseverance:** Life's challenges are inevitable, but our response to them defines our journey. Building resilience and perseverance helps us overcome obstacles and emerge stronger from adversities.

4. **Lifelong Learning:** Cultivating a mindset of lifelong learning keeps us curious, open-minded, and adaptable. It ensures we continue to grow and evolve, both personally and professionally.

Professional Excellence

1. **Leadership and Vision:** Effective leadership requires a clear vision, empathy, and the ability to inspire and guide others. Leaders who break barriers and think beyond the conventional pave the way for innovation and progress.

2. **Collaboration and Teamwork:** Success in the professional realm is often a collective effort. Collaboration and teamwork leverage diverse perspectives and skills, leading to more comprehensive and creative solutions.

3. **Ethical Practices:** Upholding integrity and ethical practices builds trust and respect in professional relationships. It creates a foundation for sustainable success and a positive organizational culture.

4. **Adaptability and Innovation:** The professional landscape is constantly changing. Being adaptable and fostering a culture of innovation ensures that individuals and organizations stay relevant and competitive.

Social Connections

1. **Empathy and Compassion:** Building meaningful social connections requires empathy and compassion. Understanding and valuing others' experiences and perspectives fosters stronger, more supportive relationships.

2. **Effective Communication:** Clear and open communication is the cornerstone of healthy relationships. It promotes understanding, resolves conflicts, and strengthens bonds.

3. **Community Engagement:** Contributing to the community and being socially responsible enhances our sense of purpose and belonging. It creates a positive impact and fosters a supportive social environment.

4. **Diversity and Inclusion:** Embracing diversity and promoting inclusion enriches our social fabric. It broadens our horizons, fosters mutual respect, and drives social progress.

Spiritual Fulfillment

1. **Inner Peace and Mindfulness:** Spiritual growth involves cultivating inner peace and mindfulness. Practices such as meditation and

reflection help us connect with our inner selves and find tranquility amidst life's chaos.

2. **Purpose and Meaning:** Discovering and pursuing our purpose gives our lives meaning. It aligns our actions with our values and aspirations, creating a sense of fulfillment and direction.

3. **Gratitude and Humility:** Practicing gratitude and humility fosters a positive outlook and a deeper appreciation for life's blessings. It nurtures contentment and fosters a sense of connection with the world around us.

4. **Transcendence and Connection:** Spiritual growth often involves transcending our individual selves and connecting with something greater. Whether through faith, nature, or the universe, this connection provides a profound sense of belonging and peace.

Conclusion

In essence, "Beyond Boundaries" has been a journey of exploring the vast potential within and around us. By embracing change, fostering self-awareness, building resilience, and committing to lifelong learning, we pave the way for personal growth. In our professional lives, visionary leadership, collaboration, ethical practices, and adaptability lead to excellence. Socially, empathy, effective communication, community engagement, and embracing diversity strengthen our connections. Spiritually, mindfulness, purpose, gratitude, and transcendence bring fulfillment and peace.

As we integrate these insights into our daily lives, we transcend our limitations and expand our horizons. We move beyond boundaries, not just as individuals, but as interconnected beings contributing to a more harmonious, innovative, and compassionate world. This is the essence of growth beyond boundaries – a continuous, holistic journey towards a more enriched and meaningful existence.

Chapter 44

BREAK YOUR OWN BOUNDARIES

In the pursuit of personal growth and self-improvement, breaking through one's own boundaries is essential. Boundaries, in this context, are the limits we place on ourselves, often unconsciously, that prevent us from reaching our full potential. These self-imposed barriers can be rooted in fear, limiting beliefs, or past experiences. To truly grow, one must challenge and transcend these boundaries. This chapter aims to guide readers through the process of identifying, challenging, and overcoming their limitations to foster personal and professional development.

Understanding Boundaries

Boundaries are the invisible lines we draw around ourselves that delineate what we believe we can and cannot achieve. They often manifest as:

Fear of Failure: Many people avoid taking risks due to the fear of failure. This fear can be paralyzing and prevent individuals from pursuing their passions or ambitions.

Limiting Beliefs: These are self-doubt and negative self-talk that convince us we are not capable of achieving more. Examples include beliefs like "I'm not good enough" or "I don't deserve success."

Comfort Zones: Comfort zones are mental and emotional spaces where we feel safe and secure. While they provide a sense of stability, they also limit our growth by discouraging us from stepping into new and challenging experiences.

Past Experiences: Previous failures or disappointments can create a mental block, leading individuals to avoid similar situations to prevent repeating past mistakes.

Identifying Personal Boundaries

The first step in breaking personal boundaries is identifying them. Reflect on the areas of your life where you feel stuck or dissatisfied. Ask yourself:

What fears are holding me back? Consider situations where you have avoided taking action due to fear.

What limiting beliefs do I hold about myself? Identify negative thoughts or beliefs that undermine your confidence.

Where do I feel too comfortable? Examine areas of your life where you might be avoiding challenges to stay in a safe, familiar space.

How have past experiences shaped my current behavior? Reflect on how past failures or setbacks may be influencing your present decisions.

Challenging Your Boundaries

Once identified, the next step is to challenge these boundaries. This involves confronting your fears and beliefs and taking proactive steps to push beyond your comfort zone.

Set Small, Achievable Goals: Begin by setting small, manageable goals that stretch your capabilities. Success in these smaller goals can build confidence and create momentum.

Embrace Failure as a Learning Opportunity: Shift your perspective on failure. Instead of viewing it as a setback, see it as a valuable learning experience that brings you closer to success.

Practice Self-Awareness and Mindfulness: Regular self-reflection and mindfulness practices can help you become more aware of your limiting beliefs and automatic responses. This awareness is crucial for making intentional changes.

Seek Support and Accountability: Surround yourself with people who encourage and support your growth. Sharing your goals with others can create a sense of accountability and provide encouragement during challenging times.

Adopt a Growth Mindset: Embrace the belief that abilities and intelligence can be developed through dedication and hard work. A growth mindset fosters resilience and a willingness to face challenges head-on.

Overcoming Obstacles

Breaking boundaries often involves encountering obstacles. These may include self-doubt, external criticism, or unforeseen challenges. Here's how to manage these obstacles effectively:

Develop Resilience: Cultivate resilience by developing coping strategies such as problem-solving skills, emotional regulation, and stress management techniques.

Reframe Negative Feedback: View criticism and setbacks as opportunities for growth rather than personal failures. Use constructive feedback to refine your approach and improve.

Stay Committed to Your Goals: Maintain focus on your long-term goals despite temporary setbacks. Persistence and commitment are key to overcoming challenges and achieving success.

Celebrating Successes

As you make progress in breaking your boundaries, it's important to celebrate your successes, no matter how small. Acknowledging your achievements reinforces positive behavior and motivates you to continue pushing your limits. Take time to reflect on how far you've come and the obstacles you've overcome.

Inspiring Others

By breaking your own boundaries, you set an example for others. Your journey of growth can inspire those around you to embark on their own path of self-improvement. Share your experiences, challenges, and triumphs to encourage and motivate others to break through their own limitations.

Conclusion

Breaking your own boundaries is a transformative journey that requires self-awareness, courage, and commitment. By identifying and challenging your fears, limiting beliefs, and comfort zones, you pave the way for personal and professional growth. Embrace the process with a growth mindset, and remember that each step forward, no matter how small, contributes to your overall development. In doing so, you not only expand your own horizons but also inspire others to reach beyond their own boundaries, creating a ripple effect of growth and achievement.

By continually pushing past your limits, you will discover new possibilities and achieve a level of personal and professional fulfillment that transcends your previous expectations. Embrace this journey of breaking boundaries, and watch as you unlock your full potential and transform your life.

Chapter 45

FINAL THOUGHTS AND MESSAGES

In the journey of personal, professional, social, and spiritual growth, we encounter countless opportunities for transformation. Each challenge, each triumph, and each setback contributes to the mosaic of our development. As we conclude this guide, it is crucial to reflect on the essence of this journey and draw inspiration from the wisdom gathered.

Embracing the Journey

Growth is not a destination but a continuous journey. It demands patience, resilience, and a willingness to adapt. Embrace each step, both the smooth and the challenging, as integral parts of your evolution. Every experience, whether positive or negative, is an opportunity to learn and grow. Understand that setbacks are not failures but stepping stones to greater achievements.

The Power of Self-Belief

One of the most significant drivers of growth is self-belief. Trust in your abilities, your vision, and your potential. This self-belief fuels perseverance and ignites the passion necessary to overcome obstacles. Remember, your inner strength is a powerful force that can propel you beyond any boundaries you perceive.

Commitment to Lifelong Learning

Personal and professional growth requires a commitment to lifelong learning. Stay curious and open-minded. Seek knowledge from diverse sources, and never stop challenging yourself. The world is ever-evolving, and so should you. Embrace new ideas, skills, and perspectives with enthusiasm and dedication.

Building Meaningful Connections

Growth is not a solitary endeavor. Building meaningful relationships and fostering connections with others enriches our journey. Surround yourself with individuals who inspire, support, and challenge you. Collaborative efforts and shared experiences enhance our growth and create a supportive network that celebrates mutual success.

Balancing Ambition with Mindfulness

While ambition drives us to achieve, mindfulness ensures that we remain grounded. Balance your aspirations with moments of reflection and self-awareness. Recognize and appreciate the present moment, and let it guide your path forward. This balance is crucial for sustained growth and overall well-being.

Making a Positive Impact

Use your growth to make a positive impact on the world around you. Whether through professional achievements, social contributions, or personal relationships, strive to leave a legacy of kindness, empathy, and excellence. Your growth should not only benefit yourself but also uplift others and contribute to the greater good.

Final Message

As you continue your journey beyond boundaries, remember that growth is a testament to your courage and perseverance. Embrace each phase with an open heart and a resilient spirit. Your potential is limitless, and every effort you make towards growth brings you closer to realizing it.

In the face of challenges, remind yourself of your strengths and past achievements. Celebrate your progress and remain focused on your goals. Your journey is unique, and every step you take is a victory in itself.

Believe in yourself, stay committed to your vision, and approach each day with optimism. The path ahead is filled with opportunities for growth and fulfillment. Embrace the adventure, and let your journey inspire others to reach beyond their own boundaries.

You have the power to transform your life and make a profound difference. Keep pushing the limits, striving for excellence, and growing in all dimensions of your being. Your journey is a beacon of possibility, and the world eagerly awaits the impact you will make.